Social Problems Series

Sheldon R. Roen, Ph.D., Editor

Behavioral Threat
and
Community Response:

A Community Psychology Inquiry

William C. Rhodes, Ph.D.

Professor of Psychology
The University of Michigan, Ann Arbor

Behavioral Publications, Inc.
New York

Library of Congress Catalog Card Number 75-174267
Standard Book Number 87705-066-X
Copyright © 1972 by **Behavioral Publications, Inc.**

BEHAVIORAL PUBLICATIONS, INC., 2852 Broadway, Morningside Heights, New York, New York 10025

Printed in the United States of America

Contents

I

The Context of Social Action

We are living in a critical period of social history. Finding that our past methods of reconciling individual and collective behavior are becoming obsolete and inadequate, we are beginning to apply new approaches and processes to the problem at accelerating rates. There is beginning a systematic examination of the nature of our present human condition and the existing armamentarium of equilibration between the individual and the community, as well as a scrutiny of the humanizing and socializing intent of this armamentarium and of some of the forces that tend to divert or deflect its purposes and results. The function and effect of schools, welfare departments, mental-health agencies, indeed, all social institutions are under searching examination. In a climate in which human thought is opening up in all directions and in which there is a revitalization of humanistic fervor in vast sectors of the population, traditional solutions and institutions no longer

1

seem appropriate. New views of social and psychological philosophy are being created, and new efforts toward a more equitable balance between individuals and their society are being made.

This powerful move to revive the dignity of life and to invest in human beings is being embodied in planned forces for the lives of individuals in collective contexts. In order that these efforts may find new ground to stand on, an open and honest examination must be undertaken of all contributors to problems of human living. Traditional dogma and beliefs about the nature of human problems must come under close scrutiny. Society's scapegoats must be looked at in a new light, and some of the displacement solutions usually inflicted on them must be revised. We must look again at what we are about in our constant constructing of new fixtures and agencies to come between us and those to whom we attribute our psychosocial ills — the mentally ill, the delinquent, the retarded, and so forth. We must take on that part of the contribution we ourselves have made to human anguish and acknowledge that much we guard against is actually our own dilemma. We must begin to recognize our own participation in the human predicament and psychosocial problems, as well as the participation of those to whom we attribute the problems and whom we consequently process into wards of the state. We have no choice but to consider solutions that not only concentrate on curing them, but on freeing ourselves as well from this mutual plight.

The Existing Situation

Any of the new social movements or community-action efforts devoted to change in the human society enters into a field of structures, rituals and forces that has been stabilized over long periods of history. No social effort begins *de novo* in a virgin action arena; rather it is forced to contend with what is already there. Such effort penetrates a crowded area of community agencies and forces that have already gained acceptance and continuity, an area that is jealous of new efforts and new competitors. The terrain, the structures and the forces seem so divisive and unrelated that a newcomer to social action assumes there is no unified framework for the human-service scene. Entering what appears to be a totally chaotic and undisciplined community mass of disparate agencies, he assumes he is coming into an area with unlimited freedom for change and competition.

To the contrary, there is a very decided order in the human-service area that has not yet been affected by new winds of social change. This order is firmly entrenched in the social body and has far-flung arteries coursing throughout. It is strongly resistant to radical change or innovation; any new social-action effort or movement that aims to influence the collective and individual psychosocial lives of the community or to influence their context must contend with this existent order. Unfortunately, a general knowledge of the existent order has never been made explicit. It has not been captured in a written conceptual schema or framework of social-action theory. There are no maps or descriptions to guide the newcomer through this terrain. What is known about the operations of the present social-service order resides in diverse individual experiences that disappear when the experienced individual fades from the scene. It must be learned over again by each individual through trial and error in the social-action scene. Except for word-of-mouth teaching or scattered fragments in the literature, there has been little effort to map the terrain.

The text of this book highlights some of the critical circumstances and conditions that exist in the social-action arena. It selects certain factors and hypothesizes others that are at work in the community to influence any course of social action.

Forces and Structures

The first section of the book formulates a general framework of the forces that guide social action. Within this framework, community action and the human drives behind it are expressed in a particular psychosocial interlock of community forces. These forces, in turn, are postulated as strongly affecting the operations of the social-action infrastructure of the community in certain wasteful directions. They have become a dominant influence in community life and have a predetermining effect on social philosophy, policy and action. They saturate all areas of psychological and sociological effort aimed at the life reciprocity between the individual and the community, and are heavily oriented to sources of behavioral threat in the community.

In the formulation of this book, the threat-oriented action forces are postulated as consisting of threat, cultural doctrine and power. The peculiar interaction of these forces, which is conjectured in this book, is perceived as creating a force field that surrounds and affects social agencies in the human-service area as they operate within the community. Under the determining influence of this special force field, it is suggested, the vast web of service agencies and systems tends to be diverted to the alleviation of threat anxiety in the culture-bearing majority and to the creation of protective barriers between this majority and certain minority groups whose culturally divergent behavior produces threat. With these circumstances operating so strongly within the community, it is difficult to move directly into any human-problem area and deal only with the crucial elements related to an apparent solution. The other factors are already there. They have existed for a long time, and it is impossible to ignore them. Any effort toward action devoted to change in the human community is swept into this special orbit. It comes under the influence of the threat-oriented force field and is immediately thrown into competition with the enduring agencies that have established long-term accommodations within this field.

The intricate web of diverse human-service agencies is conceptualized as the action instrument of massive social systems that have primary responsibility for regulating the mutuality between the individual and the community. The collection of services is described as artificially constructed coadaptation machinery designed by society to mediate between nature and nurture to form the individual and to regulate his relationship with the collective. The growth of this sprawling conglomerate is pictured as stimulated and maintained by the special field of interlocked forces described above. It has been a haphazard but precipitous growth aided by the tremendous dislocations that have taken place recently in our society. It is claimed in this book, however, that conditions have reached a point where the extensive proliferation of structures has begun to create an economic drain. There is compulsive repetition of old concepts and past solutions that are no longer applicable to current social problems. Out of this compulsive repetition there is continued mass production of like agencies having rigid and fixed boundaries that deal with peripheral psychosocial conditions, human-service stations devoted to detached, single-purpose techniques and operating on narrow segments of the human-environmental gestalt. Their use of highly focused practices and procedures aimed to affect reified names or conditions such as "delinquency" or "alcoholism" rather than broad-gauged processes that attempt to reach all psychological and sociological aspects of such conditions is viewed as increasingly ineffective. From this approach, the infrastructure has spawned more myths about human problems than it has created human solutions.

Behavior Management

The overriding social and individual purpose of this huge combine of community psychosocial forces and community agencies is construed, in the formulation of this book, as behavior management, or as adaptation of individual behavior to community requirements. The social changes occurring at such a rapid rate and the increasing difficulty of knitting the individual and the collective into a unified and mutually reinforcing fabric put new burdens on this process. The changes elevate mutual adaptation between individual and society to a cardinal position in societal values. Unless we come to terms with this process, the changes and movements at work within the society could overwhelm us.

These vaguely comprehended needs and inadequacies are claimed to be the driving force behind the current zeal for social action and change. We are becoming desperate to bring more equitable measures and solutions to the arena of psychosocial discord and disarrangement. But this alone cannot account for the great pressures to change our present human-service and human-regulation agencies. Current times have brought powerful winds of change to human thought and values. The magnitude and velocity of this change is much more than a minor effort to buttress the machinery of behavior regulation in the community. These winds will probably carry such sweeping changes in our cultural doctrine and psychosocial philosophy that minor changes in agencies will be unable to withstand them. Much broader conceptions and planning for managing the relationship between the individual and society will have to be devised before we can match these changes.

Nevertheless, an attempt is made in this book to suggest some of the approaches that might be taken to strengthen our present systems and practices. At the same time, some of the sweeping changes in philosophy and approach that are on the verge of occurring are touched upon. An attempt is made to predict some of the directions in which these changes may go in order to bring about a more balanced relationship between the individual and the collective. Finally, the last chapter of the book briefly alludes to the broader issues and revolutionary changes occurring in our society and their relationship to some of the major problems and effects on mutual adaptation between individual and community.

1

The Threat-Recoil Cycles

In this chapter we will attempt a conceptual schema of the processes and characteristics of the community directly related to behavior management. It is a tentative step toward an overall framework of the community's struggle to come to terms with the problematic human behavior and life-styles in its midst. It is not offered as a rigorous scientific model, but rather as a descriptive and conjectural starting point for further exploration. The conceptual schema attempts to examine the agencies and their institutionalized transactions that engage and control human behavior in communities. It tries to bring into its focus all of the participants in behavioral stress rather than presenting a unidimensional concentration on problematic individuals. It is not necessary for the reader to accept the particular cultural-dynamic interpretation of the book in order to consider the reciprocal nature of behavioral stress in community affairs. The empirically minded, pragmatic reader can sort out the directly denotative aspects from the more interpretive elements of the schema.

The Threat-Recoil Process

It is proposed that there is a more or less constant and steady state of uneasiness in the community arising from the potential divergence of individual behavior or life-styles from collective needs or requirements. Periodically this disquiet breaks above the surface of normal psycho-social equilibrium and becomes evident in more profound stress cycles sweeping across the community. Such cycles can develop a velocity that creates upset and agitation across the nation and involves major segments of the population in their turbulence.

The cycles are precipitated by an incipient or actual behavioral threat from a minority population segment that arouses concern and recoil in the majority of the population. Within any single significant local, state or national threat-recoil cycle, we can observe a gradual community awakening to the behavioral threat that is spreading in ever-expanding ripples across the community. The ripples gradually form a wave pattern, and this wave of concern begins to build in intensity across the community or nation. We can observe an accelerated increase of upset and agitation, and eventually this alarm may be raised to the level of panic. The waves then toss the community or nation into a series of urgent actions and reactions. Gradually over an interval of time, we can observe the weakening of the wave pattern, a subsiding of the emotions and emergency actions; with the gradual diminution of community alarm, there is also fading of the community's preoccupation or obsession with the particular human behavior or style of living that aroused the alarm.

If we study a local segment of the cycle, we can watch the community suddenly become aroused over a specific behavior, child abuse, for instance, or alcoholism, or mental illness. We can then observe an eruption of agitated exchanges in the community and see a variety of remedial plans put forward and translated into action. Then, as the cycle runs its course, we see the public turn its excitement and its resources to a new source of threat, a new provocative behavior. This time it may be sexual perversion, gang activity, murder or whatever human condition happens to be singled out as a threshold danger to the society at that moment in time. The focus of the upset shifts from year to year, but the threat-recoil process seems to be a constantly recurring part of community life.

The Activator

The community threat-recoil cycle can begin with either overt behavior or with warnings of its imminence. The precipitant is the individual or group that emits threatening behavior or exists in one of the many human-predicament states challenging our culture. This could be alcoholism, drug addiction, retardation, sexual deviation, delinquency, mental illness, underachievement, and so on.

When the threat-recoil cycle is precipitated by overt behavior, the quality of the cycle seems influenced by certain characteristics of the behavior. For instance, the intensity, extensiveness and duration of community recoil seem to be determined by such behavioral characteristics as 1) frequency of occurrence, 2) place in the hierarchy of cultural taboos, 3) intensity of behavior, 4) degree of visibility in the open community, 5) geographical location and distribution in the community, and 6) the drama of the circumstances. A very dramatic occurrence of even a single instance of culturally prohibited behavior is sufficient to precipitate intense recoil. A teen-gang killing of a rival gang member on the steps of a church or in a school yard or the killing of a priest or rabbi in an attempted mugging is enough to produce such a cycle.

The politician and the professional frequently assume responsibility for searching out incipient threats in the society and presenting research data, surveys and conceptualizations that serve to symbolize an occurrence of threat. These symbolizations are capable of producing the same effect as the real occurrence: professional warnings can substitute for threatening behavior in producing community alarm and community action. The report of a national commission for instance, can produce the same kind of upset and concern as the direct experience of a profound incident of gang fighting. The politician and professional also unwittingly play other roles in precipitation of a threat-recoil cycle. They frequently point out nonvisible behavior that is provocative and that violates important cultural prohibitions; they also find ways of raising the cultural awareness of these behaviors to the point where they become known and produce the same impact as more readily observed threatening human expressions. In this case, unlike the above potential behavior, the culturally tabooed expressions are occurring in the life of the community, but they are not observable, and therefore will not produce threat until they are called to the attention of the community. A current example of this is the professional attempt to raise the visibility of suicide and thus motivate the community to support suicide-prevention programs.

The community has begun to depend on professionals and politicians to monitor social affairs and detect possible threats to collective life. To an important extent, therefore, the community has come to rely on them for early warning and interpretation of the nature of threat toward which the community should direct its concern. More and more, such warnings have become as effective in instigating a threat-recoil cycle as directly observable tabooed behavior. With the proliferation of agencies and professionals with a commitment to studying individual divergence, and with the significant part that threat and recoil play in political affairs, the rate of warnings has continued to grow. Furthermore, as mass communication has improved and as the transactional-recoil process has become institutionalized in the community, it is logical to infer that monitoring will become more significant in the social order.

Definitions of the Threat

The way in which the threat is defined, the language that is used, is borrowed from the very societal agencies that have grown up around the collective need to reconcile claims of self with claims of society. One precipitating behavior may be defined with the language of mental health, another with the terminology of public welfare, and still another may be borrowed from the legal-correctional system. No matter which language the threatened public sector chooses, the professional groups associated with the various agencies and socializing institutions will reconceptualize the provocative behavior into its own terms, its own concepts, theories, technologies and operational patterns. Community consensus on the name of the turbulence focus will thus be redefined and redistributed across the many human-service groups concerned with the behavioral affairs of the community. For instance, acting-out behavior involving violation of others' health or property rights may be defined as "delinquency" in legal-correctional terms, as "character disorder" or "sociopathic behavior" in mental-health jargon, or may be defined in educational or social-welfare vocabulary as "maladjustment." The public is dependent on the language systems developed by these agencies to describe what is threatening.

The cluster of events and general climate at the time of the occurrence of a threat usually determines which of these agency languages is most likely to be used to describe the threat. For instance, if there is a particularly dynamic and well-liked psychiatrist in a community at the time that a wanton sexual attack is committed, and the newspaper has just completed a series of exposé articles on the condition of the local mental hospital, the psychiatrist is likely to be asked to define the meaning of the sexual attack. In this situation, the language used in the recoil cycle following from the sexual attack is likely to be the language of mental health. The provoking behaviors, therefore, will be given additional and even superfluous meaning in terms of the concepts, language and interpretations of human behavior that the various socializing agents have established over the years.

The public is very fickle with its loyalty to terms and agencies, shifting its interest and commitment from one system to another. At one time it may favor the language and agency patterns of mental health, and at another time it may translate all of its alarms into the language of education. Only the range of institutionalized agencies of socialization existing in a particular society limits its shifting affections.

An Interlock of Community Interactions

The cyclic process of threat and recoil that mobilizes community defenses has become a ritual of roles played out by three major groups within the community: 1) the minority group of threat exciters, 2) the majority group of threat responders, and 3) the appropriate power structures of the community. These three groups do not interact directly; rather the ritual of their group roles is mediated through the agencies and systems of the community that have responsibility for regulating behavioral threat. This includes legal-correction, social-welfare, education, mental-health and other behavioral systems. When murmurs of apprehension over a particular culturally prohibited behavior begin to spread horizontally through community members, the threat also begins to engage community power structures and to move upward through the various layers of the power pyramid. The greater the number of individual community members who become agitated over the threat, the higher up the power pyramid it travels. At this point, concerted pressure from the threat-responder group begins to assume political and economic importance, and the upper power levels of local, state and/or national government are forced into action. We have seen this occur in crime and delinquency, in mental health and, more recently, in student unrest.

The minority group whose pattern of life and behavior the collective considers dangerous becomes the exciter of intense emotion and defensive reactions from the majority of the general public. Under the circumstances, the minority exciter group and its behavior is frequently cut off from normal communication with the majority population and regular channels of social intercourse. Special channels of communication and societal devices are maneuvered between the rest of the community and these exciters. These devices may be community buffer zones like those that surround slums. They may also be programs of agencies and institutions that come between majority and minority groups. Under the influence of threat-recoil pressures, the behavioral-regulator functions of the agencies and institutions are frequently diverted to that of permanent buffer or separator between threat responders and exciters. Much of the energy of these agencies is directed toward reduction of anxiety in the threat responders. Police agencies continually reassure the public that it is being defended against crime. Mental-health agencies spend an inordinate amount of time and personnel on public relations, community education and so forth. The same pressures maintain a special set of transactions among the threat responders, threat exciters and power structures.

It is recognized that threat is not the only dimension governing the transactions among those classified into the three sectors of exciters, responders and power structures. There are many transactional dimensions, many positive exchanges and many interactions that will not be treated in this book. Instead, this special set of threat-recoil transactions will be separated from the total community functioning and examined in microcosm. They will be studied because of the light they throw on the functions of the community systems that regulate collective behavior.

Psychosocial Functioning of the Triad

Let us turn now to a conceptualization of the roles and relationships played out in the community by the previously identified trio of threat exciters, responders and power structures. We will deliberately restrict our conceptualization to the dynamic exchanges among these as they are governed by psychosocial threat. We will further limit our consideration of this trio by confining our examination to their dynamic interactions with the behavioral agencies and institutions in the community. From this referent base we might look upon the threatening sector as being composed of all types of tabooed groups in the society. We may look upon the threat-responding majority of the community as the social group enjoying something of a protectorate status under behavioral agencies and power structures. Let us examine each of these groups.

The Threatening Sector

All of the groups who produce threatening behavior, whose life-style is threatening, or who inhabit distressed areas within the community might be classed together in this tabooed sector. They are special kinds of minority groups that the community responds to primarily on the basis of their threatening characteristics. In the relationship of the community to any member of this group, the particular disturbing behavioral category or life-style governs and takes precedence over all other possible relationships. The minority-group member is reacted to as an "alcoholic," as "mentally ill," as a "retardate," a "delinquent," or a "deviate"; in other words, the community orients itself around his threatening categorical classification. He thus becomes an irritant against which the community must construct insulating layers. The community's reaction is specific. There are mental hospitals for the "mentally ill," prisons for the criminal, and so on; but the insulating or protective maneuvers are fairly general toward all threatening members, for example, isolation, exile, extrusion.

The Threat-Reactive Sector

The public, or threat-reactive sector, is made up largely of the vast mass of individuals who constitute the base group of our society. The culture bearers of society, this group constitutes the other side of the threatening relationship. This middle group is most vulnerable to loss of social and economic status and therefore is more cautious and circumspect with regard to its own behavior and that of others.

It is against the standard of this middle group that all threatening groups are measured and defined. Its consensus determines what is outside the realm of "acceptable behavior." Its trained recoil locates and exposes the threat provokers. Its joint appeal for protection, or its composite acceptance of the offer of protection from power and agency groups, specifies which individuals and which groups will be classified as threatening.

From the threat-recoil frame of reference suggested in this chapter, we might describe this group as the most successful segment of society in both dodging and detecting public taboo and threat. This group stays out of trouble and therefore carries greatest weight with the trouble-handling machinery of the society. Individuals in this group generally manage to avoid placement in such threatening categories as mental illness, mental retardation, delinquency, suicide, drug addiction, sexual deviance, social maladjustment, social withdrawal, cultural dis-advantagement, underachievement and drop out.

A special type of social skill is required to elude all of these categories. The countless culturally threatening behaviors and the endless possibilities for tabooed forms of human existence make successful performance in the community, under normal conditions, a very precarious endeavor, even for members of culturally advantaged groups. There are so many cultural reefs on which a member of society can run aground, so many unmarked social lines on which the individual can lose his balance, so many undesirable minority classifications that he can so easily fall into that only the most skilled can traverse the difficult yet "socially acceptable" terrain. Thus to be publicly free of taint the individual has to be highly competent in detecting and diverting any appearance of threat. It is a type of competency that calls for meticulous training from the earliest years. In this accomplishment the individual must develop high sensitivity in detecting cues and signals of threatening characteristics within himself, others and surrounding circumstances. He must also develop skills in minimizing such cues in the presentation of himself and in his private living, which influences this public presentation. He must, in other words, orient a major segment of his life around minimizing threatening aspects of his conduct and avoiding conditions and behaviors that produce threat.

In order to become selectively sensitive to detection and avoidance of the vital cues involved, the individual must master the data bank of threats that his culture has built up over centuries and learn this vast catalogue and incorporate it within himself, detecting even the most obscure specimens of the catalogue in himself and in others.

The individual not only has to play many roles in his life, but his everyday life is surrounded by many shifting exigencies and undergoes many changing internal states. In order to remain in the acceptable class, therefore, he has to spend a great amount of time and energy in monitoring threat and coping with the danger it presents in himself and in his community image.

Let us take the single category of "emotional distur- bance" for instance. There are so many states of being, so many conditions of behavior and such a multiplicity of definitions of this category that one finds it difficult to set up criteria for exclusion from the group. Even the most serious manifestation of this term, "mental illness," has no single definition and lacks clear-cut characteristics. There is certainly no scientific consensus regarding who is mentally ill and who isn't. Several reviews of the professional literature dealing with the definition of this concept conclude that there is no agreement as to what constitutes mental illness. And yet, as a category, this term arouses powerful emotions within the threat-responsive general public.

There are many ways in which a person may slip into this category. A psychological test battery can determine it or a group of one's peers or supervisors. A public consensus or legal process can class an individual as disturbed. A voluntary or involuntary involvement with a particular agency process, such as being hospitalized in a mental hospital or seeking psychiatric help, can do this. William Scott's (1958) careful review of research definitions of mental illness lists each of these indexes and provides more detail on the inadequacies of each definition. The reader is referred to his article for a more complete treatment of the problem.

With this example of the single category of mental illness and an awareness of all the other categories always open and possible for any member of the community, let us return to our general statement. The protectorate group involved in the threat-recoil analysis presented here could be thought of as the individuals most skilled in avoiding threatening classifications. (Though let us hasten to add that this group also has many characteristics and skills that are constructive and nonreactive to threat.) When threat is aroused within this group, it turns to the appropriate power, political and professional groups of the community for relief from and attention to the threatening source. The dimension of their lives being singled out here is the threat-dominated aspect of their functioning and psychosocial relationships.

The Power Structure

The power structures of the community are not a monolithic framework, rather there are many differing power structures depending on the sphere of influence at stake. Here we are talking about a particular decision-making sector, about the administrative, judicial and legislative bodies of various governing units as they relate to behavioral agencies; in addition we are referring to the group made up of the influential community members and boards that control agency service or caretaking institutional functioning. When the power structure is moved by threat-recoil cycles and engages the services of the behavioral agencies and institutions such as social welfare, education and mental health, it creates a particular alliance. This alliance is oriented to threat reduction and threat mediation. Because of its tendency of this alliance to be acutely aware of and influenced by the pressures of psychosocial threat, it might be looked upon as a protectorate sector as well as the behavior-regulator sector of the community.

The role of the protectorate sector

The role professionals and politicians play in transactions revolving around psychosocial or behavioral threat may be described as predominantly that of social protector. The functional social role of this sector is ordinarily somewhat variable. It may fluctuate from caretaker of the troubled to rigid enforcer of cultural prohibitions. The probability of the cultural-enforcement role tends to be accentuated under the prod of the threat-recoil process. Since power structures are quite sensitive to public pressure, governing groups are quite likely to move to reinforce the constraints that threat-responsive groups demand.

The operational patterns and programs (e.g., clinics, detention centers, day-care programs) of behavioral systems and agencies are ordinarily less responsive to public pressure. Ideally, these operational patterns and programs are not mere political instruments, but rather perform the objective function of modulating the stresses and strains among the threat exciters, responders and power structures. In terms of funding and authority, however, these systems are maintained in a direct-line relationship to the governing bodies. Therefore in times of stress when threat and recoil intensify, their position is something less than free and uncommitted in the power realm. Ideally there should be enough detachment and versatility for them to be able to support or succor whichever sector requires the greatest buttressing under the circumstances. Since threat increases the gravitational pull into the orbit of government and public interests, their multiple alliances are more likely to resolve themselves in the direction of a coalition with government and political operations in behalf of the majority group.

Within the atmosphere of threat 1) the decision-making or power segment (particularly in the judicial, legislative and executive branches of government) and 2) professionals and agencies form a loosely organized coalition that can move in several directions to reduce tension. These directions might include maneuvering a single agency into position to mediate between the community and the discordant individuals who are perceived as producing the threat. They might consist of creating a new agency or a new constellation of forces to control or contain the behavior that is alarming, or might be a different way of deploying several existing agencies to deal with the problem. Whatever the maneuver, the necessity to appropriate or disburse community, state or federal funds to meet the threat accompanies it. In these circumstances, the power structures (and indirectly, the agencies) that are pressured to make these decisions are also provided with fresh or renewed access to a certain portion of the community economy. Thus community alarm contributes two sources of power renewal for both the political and the professional groups: 1) a source arising out of the public sanction to levy and disburse funds, and 2) a source arising out of collective need for psychological protection from threat. In this sense, then, it might be said that individual human divergence in the community provides one of the sources for sustaining and renewing power in that group already occupying the power position.

Furthermore, recurrent behavioral threat also serves to maintain the reciprocal protector-protectorate relationship between the behavioral agencies and the threat-reactive public segment. In the process of community arousal over culturally discordant behavior, various organized groups such as civic associations, church associations and women's clubs begin to demand that community authorities take action. Petitions are signed, statements released to the newspapers, television interviews sought, editorials written. The buildup of public pressure begins to be felt by the informal power groups associated with behavioral threat, and these structures begin to focus on the mayor's office or the office of the county commissioners, or the governor, or the president to provide additional funds and authority to behavioral agencies such as public-welfare or corrective mental-health organizations.

Threat, power and the protector coalition

The constant reactivation of the protector-protectorate relationship serves to maintain the coalition between power segments of communities and the behavioral systems. It also sustains that part of the apparatus and operational delivery patterns that was developed to process, maintain and regulate community behavior according to cultural standards. This is particularly true for the agencies that are partially or fully financed with public funds and devote their energies to threat control. The systems that we have in mind here are exemplified in such realms as legal correction, social welfare, education and medical/mental health. The agencies or operational patterns of these systems are integral parts of government at local, state and national levels. As these agencies have responded to the threat-recoil phenomena of society, they have become more and more closely linked to government. Such a reciprocity has developed between the two bodies that government and institutions are frequently perceived by the threat-responsive public masses as a single body.

The public, however, makes a differentiation between the two bodies with regard to their respective protective powers. The power segment is perceived as the mover of community forces, and professionals in the socializing systems are credited with a different sort of power. In the eyes of the community, these professionals are capable of deciphering the mysteries of alarming behaviors and transforming them into safe and acceptable human-cultural patterns. They are capable of exerting the force and creating the paraphernalia for controlling both discordance and threat.

With the ascription of these powers to government and socializing agencies by the general public under conditions of threat and recoil, it is possible for abuses to occur. Under threat, every one of the behavioral systems is likely to concentrate on the particular problem or condition that is arousing the community, frequently diverting many of its resources for human construction and development to control and reduction of threat. A resulting state of turbulence encourages wasteful competitiveness among the systems and jockeying for positions that will assure assignment of the problem to their jurisdiction. It is also possible for the power segment to turn the threat into the service of a vested political need that exists at that moment. For instance, when an election is a stake, the threat could be redefined in party terms quite peripheral to the nature of the perceived threat. We might say, therefore, that the threat provoker can be used as an instrument for aggrandizement of a behavioral system or a political party. While in many cases such use of the threatening groups as a public issue for the furtherance of a political or system's end may be quite justified, there is always the danger of abuse of the least protected and most helpless segments of our society. Such possible abuse leads both the threatening sector and the power structures to their own dehumanization and to that of the other segments of the community participating in the affair. We must, therefore, be cognizant of these possibilities and guard against frequency of their occurrence.

Explanatory Constructions

The Psychocultural Nature of Threat

A number of logical explanations can be employed to account for the amount of community concern that can be aroused by certain behaviors and habits of living. In this section we will draw on some of the psychological explanations that depict cultural and social processes as being constructed out of human urges and impulses. We will move from a base of such postulates toward the descriptive constructions of the first part of the chapter.

The construction offered here is one of cultural relativity, plus the mutual incompatibility between certain human individual impulses on the one hand and the requirements for collective living on the other. These incompatibilities between individual and social claims are depicted as being complicated by the cultural frame of reference that guides so much of human conduct. Some of the more or less natural antipathies between individual urges and social claims would inevitably produce stress in human environments. It is suggested, however, that this strain is exaggerated by the accumulation of cultural taboos that have been handed down from generation to generation to contemporary society. This repository of restrictive "rules" contributes significantly to the detonating capacity of certain life-styles, behaviors or behavior settings. Cultural taboos have grown out of the awareness of the inevitable discontinuities between individuals and society. Historically, society has been so sensitive to this antithesis that it has built a vast collection of coded sanctions. This repository remains active and guides the defensive overreaction of the community to a vast array of human behavioral and life-habit manifestations.

In this construction, it is argued that much of the quality of behavior regarded as threatening arises from this cultural-repository overlay. The threatening sector of the community might be thought of as reflecting that part of the individual's makeup that may be antithetical to collective living, but this is greatly magnified by such an overlay. On the other hand, the threat-responder sector represents that major segment of society that has incorporated the cultural repository into its psychosocial functioning. We could think of this overlay of real and imagined behavioral threats as actually propelling these threat-recoil cycles and exchanges between the threat-exciters, responders and power groups. *We might think of the threat-aroused roles of the interacting trio as reflecting the efforts of the human being to accommodate to society.*

The threatening sector of the community reflects, in social form, that part of the individual that is either actually or conceptually antithetical to collective life and that part of the individual that bears the burden of self-denial in behalf of group living. The power structure is the arbiter of judgment and accommodation. The sectors can be viewed as representing man's ceaseless struggle to reconcile these contending claims for his loyalty and his periodic effort to resolve his dilemma by trying to escape either himself or his culture. There is a constant strain of what man is against what the culture says he ought to be. The strain is unnecessarily increased by the fact that although the measure of "ought to be" shifts and changes with each historical period, the culture seldom drops any of these measures from its repository. Through time, community culture has banked an overwhelming accumulation of such measures of man. This burden becomes almost intolerable for many of us, making community life an unnecessarily labored passage because of this interaction of cultural taboos with man's repertory for states of being and boundless capacity for fear. There are so many things that each individual *is* that he *ought not to be*. In his lifetime he lives many experiences that he ought not to live if he obeys the tyranny of the questionable part of the historical repository of culture. As an individual he is helpless before this repository because there are no institutionalized means for periodic reexamination of the functional utility of even the most archaic of these deposits. Therefore, we carry a vast, indiscriminate mass of cultural taboos that we must live with. This repository continually upsets the balance between society's accommodation to man and man's accommodation to it. Placing a handicap on the individual, it frequently requires more adaptation from the individual than from the society. The individual is forced to accommodate to social systems and social structures under certain aspects of this surplus repository, rather than society's searching for ways to modify social systems to fit greater ranges of individual variation. Under the influence of this repository the living structures of society are unnecessarily rigid and impervious to variability in individual behaviors and states of being.

Each of the separate items in this cumbersome accumulation of man's psychocultural history is highly charged with emotion and laden with qualities of taboo. Because of the nature of man, each one of the culturally prohibited behaviors could easily be exercised by every individual in the society. The individual who has transferred these restrictions out of the storehouse of culture into his own memory bank is always conscious of this possibility. Therefore, he carries around within himself not only the burdensome load of the internalized repository, but also the loaded threat of his own behavioral tendencies that can violate these taboos. To this extent, his actions and potential actions are perpetually fraught with danger. This places an unnecessary cloud over his community life that makes his passage tense and hazardous, creating obstacles to relaxed and free expression and keeping him constantly on guard against these dangers.

The threat exciters, therefore, by acting out culturally illicit behaviors and tabooed states, express openly a threat that is constantly trembling as a potential in the behavioral repertory of the threat avoiders. Public attention and communication about the expressed behavior further activate the mass and set off a vast cycle of recoil that reverberates throughout the community. When protective sectors of society begin to move facilities, installations, programs and behavior mediators into the arena of turbulence, the threat-reactive public is momentarily reassured. Thus the intensity of this particular threat is regarded as diminished.

Not all individual threats to collective life are necessarily fantasied, because there is real incompatibility between certain of the individual and social claims. The extent of threat from individual behavior, however, has become highly exaggerated because of the sediment of archaic deposits of taboo that has settled into our society. This explanatory construction, of course, is only one of many alternative explanations. Many reasons could be offered for the extent to which this country involves itself in one massive and widespread behavior-control program after another and seems to be involved in an obsessive expansion of agency resources. This type of generalization, however, might have functional utility for the nation's domestic affairs. This utility would exist in the extent to which prevailing conceptions and practices in unresolved human-problem areas might be modified or redirected. If we could view a part of human pathology as a reciprocal participation involving not only the divergent individual but also the mass of individuals who are reactive to such divergence, then it is quite possible that our social solutions might assume new dimensions.

2

The Exciter and the Responder

The key to the tumultuous social process that mobilizes and maintains many human-service programs lies, to a major extent, in the relationship between community exciters and responders. Therefore this chapter will center on the reciprocity of this interaction. Since we are concentrating on the threat-recoil cycles and their relationship to community action and the activities of social agencies, we will present a single-dimensional view focused on the discordance of their mutual interactions. The disjunctive and disordered aspect of the relationship will be separated from the total picture. This admittedly presents an exaggerated description, because the view is microcosmic and thus magnified many times by its separation from the whole, which includes such ameliorating qualities as love, concern, constructive urges and wisdom. But for purposes of understanding this particular set of forces bearing on the community programming, we will put aside the whole and concentrate on this particular disjunctive segment. Perhaps by lifting out this disease between the two sectors, we can see more clearly what our tasks are in the process of managing human behavior.

When looking at the operations of community agencies, we are concerned with masses of individuals and large ecological units. The social agencies' major behavior-regulator and behavior-control programs must address themselves to these masses and to their collective reciprocities. Therefore we should return to the population sectors that we labeled the threatening and threat-responder classes. We will try to describe their mutually provocative characteristics and the distinctive differences in characteristics of their environmental habitats.

A Psychological Class System

There seems to be a relationship between socioeconomic class and membership in either the threat-elicitor or threat-responder class. In other words, there appears to be a psychological dimension related to the social and economic dimension. Although this is not a perfect relationship, the psychologically disturbable class seems to come largely from the middle socioeconomic class and the most psychologically disturbing group seems to come largely from the lowest socioeconomic class.

Characteristics of the Threat-Exciter Class

Psychological vulnerability
Some of our present ecological, epidemiological and demographic data focuses upon the psychological vulnerability of the lower socioeconomic strata of the com-

munity. These groups are particularly vulnerable to estrangement and to classification in one of the discordant or pathological categories of the tabooed class. This conclusion is supported by studies in mental illness (Marc Fried, 1964; Faris and Dunham, 1939; Hollingshead and Redlich, 1953; Mischler and Scotch, 1963), delinquency (Shaw and McKay, 1942; Lander, 1954; Morris, 1958; Jephcott and Carter, 1954), mental retardation (Jenkins and Brown, 1935; Butler and Gibson, 1954; Mercer, 1965), as well as studies of many other discordant, deviant or pathological behaviors.

In general, individuals in this sector openly expose those individual qualities of human nature that are either fully renounced or carefully hidden by the threat-responder class. They frequently act out impulses that are unacceptable to the threat-responder group and exhibit these behaviors openly on the streets. They usually inhabit enclaves or ghettos within the community, and their family boundaries are usually weak or extremely permeable. They are not conditioned to the total psychological ideology of our society, which includes the delay of gratification, the focal importance of work and production, the inviolable nature of property, the psychological denial of aggression, the limited expression of sex, the suppression of play, the ascendancy of the reality principle over the pleasure principle, the superiority of reason, and the danger of irrationality.

Family structure

Within the threat-exciter group there are high rates of one-parent families. It could be argued that a large proportion of these families are really pseudofamilies and are in a sense jerry-built facsimiles of modal family units in American communities (jerry-built in the sense that they have been artificially and precariously maintained by public welfare programs). The family structure is always in jeopardy, and there is a high probability that many of them would collapse as units without outside support. The pseudo families are held together, to a large extent, in "female-based" households. Although there may be relatively strong interpersonal attachments within the group, continuity of direct person-to-person contact within the household is frequently sporadic and unstable. Such families lack the community linkages that, in the middle class, are forged through step-by-step reconciliation between individual claims and social claims. Such a process of culture molding is generally haphazard and inconsistent for the threat-exciter group. The parent figure assumes very little social authority and has little skill or confidence as a social teacher. As Hyland Lewis (1960) has pointed out, the parent loses his control as a socializing agent at a very early stage in the child's life history. Because it fails to discharge the very specific community-deputized function of the family, this type family is a very poor transmission agent for the modal culture of the society. The parent lacks the culturally tempered cognitive tools, understandings, behavioral repertoires, emotional controls and relationship skills required by our culture. Furthermore, parent figures lack the important psychosocial repressions that are so typical of the modal social group. Such parent figures cannot provide the identification image of an adequately repressed, psychologically skilled, culturally wise community model. They do not have internalized replicas of the external socializing structures, and therefore the culture cannot pass through their own systems to be transmitted to the child, as happens with more thoroughly acculturated parents.

Although this type of family begins like modal families as a biosocial and psychosocial unit, the union is short-lived. The biological parents, unlike the modal family, usually do not maintain the social appearances of permanent or relatively exclusive sexual union. Further, they do not provide a continuous bridge between the child and such community organizations as 1) the economic systems of work and productive structures, taxing structures, 2) the formal power systems of political or government structures, and other informal power structures, 3) the human-behavior-mediating network of systems and agencies, primarily educational, that is responsible for binding the chronology of individual and of community into a single history. The most direct structural tie of the pseudo family to the community is through emergency, periodic or custody-taking organizations such as legal correction or social welfare. In spite of being compelled to submit their young to the acculturation forces of the school, the parent figures have little control over the schools and lack a common ground on which to relate family processes to school processes or cultural transmission.

The larger community requires a family to be an economically productive unit. It also expects the parents to transmit work-achievement and economic-production values to the child. The whole economic apparatus is geared to this orientation. The pseudo family, however, is an economically dependent rather than an economically productive unit. It usually has only marginal interest in the techniques and organizations of work and production. The pseudo family is further disadvantaged by the large proportion of female-based households. In our society, the female has second-class citizenship and a second-class role as a direct participant in the economic structures of our society. This is also true in the political-power field.

Even more important is the perpetual psychological threat of members of these families to the community at large. The individuals do not learn effective control or subjugation of their impulses, which are unhesitatingly expressed in their overt behavior. From the frame of reference of the large threat-responder sector of the community, such families are half-civilized. They have not effectively learned the vast lexicon of cultural taboos and legends that have accumulated through the centuries or the art of public presentation of themselves so as to reduce cultural threat in their posture and behavior. In the free expression of their tabooed behavior they establish a living tradition for their children that is as influential as any tradition transmission in any group. In their behavioral expression they are a link to the threat provokers of the future. Their legacy to the community is a progeny that will be almost identical to themselves.

Behavior in the streets

In openly expressing culturally illicit behaviors, this group mobilizes the threat-responder class. The most disturbing behavior is that which is expressed freely on the streets where community life is lived. Hence the behavior on the street appears to have the greatest potential to frighten and upset the community. The street is public, and the public display of tabooed behavior threatens to make it part of life. Openness gives such behavior an actuality and carries the threat of public acceptance and approval. It is feared that such a foothold will be enlarged to wider sectors of community existence, causing the influence to spread and reach out to awaken traitorous impulses within all of us. With increased density of population there is an increase in probability of illicit behavior's issuing onto the streets. Until more boundaries are erected to contain the behaviors and halt their spread to surrounding geographical areas, more and more cycles of threat recoil are likely to make their appearance.

The habitat zones

The streets on which these illicit behaviors are openly displayed themselves become tabooed areas. For the psychologically threatened class they become zones that require isolation, avoidance and protective encirclements. Stronger restraints are placed around them. They become completely enclosed by invisible but real social, economic, power and psychological barriers. They become exile islands within the larger community. The inhabitants of these encircled enclaves acquire a general stamp of community exclusion. The opportunity structures of the community usually stop at the borders; the schools within them are very frequently second-rate. Children from these zones who go to outside schools are just as frequently looked down upon and rejected by teachers and students alike. The police are usually either very harassing or afford little protection to the area's inhabitants (at least this is the perception that the inhabitants have of police forces).

Typically the neighborhoods are deteriorating and disorganized, with little home ownership. They usually merge with heavy industrial sections. There are dense concentrations of population, with many single dwellings being occupied by more than one family and with each room of multiple dwellings overflowing with inhabitants. These are typically the receiving areas for the immigration of displaced groups like rural migrants to urban areas and for special isolates like the restless, drifting middle-aged males who lost their way somewhere in their early lives. In the United States, such neighborhoods are the semipermanent habitat for specific culturally stagnant groups such as Negroes, Mexicans and Puerto Ricans. They are settlements for major waves of immigrants from foreign lands.

In this part of the community, organized vice, crime, and so forth occur to a greater extent than in other areas.

The age of recruitment into the discordant constituency is younger than the age of community offenders in other parts of the city. Their initiation into containment and correctional agencies is earlier than for other populations. The quality of their discordant behavior seems to be more serious, more intensive, more frequent and more alarming than for other population groups. Individuals from this source of recruits to the discordant categories are recidivists in many areas of discordance (like delinquency) and are likely to exhibit multiple types of discordant behavior as a way of life.

Source spring of threat

These families and exile zones are breeding pools for individual psychological discordance of all types that threatens the concept of social order held by the larger community. They are also the induction and recruiting centers for a steady supply of community isolates. Although these families and centers are not the only source of psychological threat to the community, they are the most visible areas where almost any kind of individual psychological discordance that can be named is found to collect in major aggregates, including schizophrenia, delinquency, alcoholism, drug addiction and overt sexual acting out.

Characteristics of the Threat-Responder Class

Note of caution

The following discussion of the threat-responder class, like the previous discussion of the threatening class, will seem to concentrate too heavily on negative characteristics. It must be remembered that the cross section of human affairs being examined here is extracted from the distortions of the threat-recoil process. Therefore the presentation deals with the negative or pathological aspects of society that distort the positive, constructive qualities of modern life. It does not deny the strengths and virtues of the group being examined but merely takes these for granted, holds them aside, and goes on to examine the negative aspects of this modal psychological class as they reflect the negative qualities of the estranged class.

Just as the descriptive characteristics of the threat-exciter group was said to frequently converge with the characteristics of the lower socioeconomic strata, those of the threat-responder group are frequently convergent with the elements of the socioeconomic middle class of our society. This description, however, will be more directly related to the psychological base of this group rather than to its socioeconomic base. Many of the lower socioeconomic class fit into this group, just as many middle class fit into the threat-exciter group. An oversimplified generalization might say that we witness in the threat-exciter class a strong presentation of individual claims, impulses, desires and separateness against the claims and demands of the society. On the other hand, in the responder class there might be said to be a stronger identification with the claims, demands and renunciations of the collective form of existence.

In this particular section the detracting elements of the threat-responder group that help create states of pathology will be intensified and highlighted. If they are overemphasized or biased, it is hoped that they are not psychologically invalid.

Ideology

Many behavioral scientists and philosophers have pointed to the Protestant-Christian-Judaic ethic as characterizing the dominant culture of the United States. Included are such concepts as delay of gratification, importance of work and production, inviolate nature of property, denial of aggression and the body, denial of death, suppression of play, ascendancy of the reality principle over the pleasure principle, and superiority of reason and danger of irrationality. In terms of the threat-recoil construction offered in the second chapter, these are the guiding principles and identifying characteristics of the threat-responder or the strained group of the society. Expressive manifestations of the exciter group are seen by the responders as threatening to the social order and therefore threatening to themselves.

Descriptive characteristics

If we look for enumerative or descriptive characteristics, the literature of the behavioral sciences is relatively silent in respect to this culture-bearing group. We could assume that this group provides the normative criterion for our society and could say that they are distinct from the threat exciters in the absence of the descriptive characteristics that have already been summarized for the threat-exciter group. For instance, they hold majority- rather than minority-group membership. In the United States they are, by and large, white, Protestant, at least second- or third-generation citizens, and high-school or college educated. As a group, they have relatively good physical health, with low infant-mortality and tuberculosis rates. There are few instances of schizophrenia, delinquency, homicides, desertions, etc. Since their legal infractions are relatively minor, they make up a relatively low proportion of prison populations.

The habitat

In contrasting the environment or neighborhood setting of this group with the threatening sector, we can say that most of its members in this country are of the middle class in socioeconomic status and live in geographical areas of high home ownership, few rooming houses, few single houses with multiple family units, and very little industry. There is very little turbulence or tabooed behavior on their streets. The population density is relatively low; there are no restrictive boundaries around these community sections, and the inhabitants move freely in and out of the neighborhood. There are few police in evidence, and police contact with the inhabitants of these sections is somewhat friendly and deferent.

Family structure

The units are usually two-parent families and are relatively stable. This large middle-class portion is frequently referred to as the base-line group for psychological normality and family life, and yet this is the segment of society that has been so thoroughly mined in the clinical literature of psychopathology. If we were allowed to generalize from this literature, we might be tempted to conclude that these family units are hotbeds of neuroticism. They would appear to be laden with pathological relationships with many types of subtle internal family constraints and abrasions and with internal hostilities that take bizarre and strange shapes, which hide themselves in the offices of private physicians and psychiatrists, private hospitals and private homes.

Economic description

Economically, this is a socially contributing sector with firm commitments to work and industry. They usually learn marketable skills and are steadily employed over long periods of their lives; they are insured against periods of unemployment or reduced income. From very early life they shape themselves into instruments of production that willingly participate in and maintain the economy of the community. Yet, according to Herbert Marcuse:

For the vast majority of the population, the scope and mode of
satisfaction are determined by their own labor; but their labor is
work for an apparatus which they do not control, which operates as
an independent power to which individuals must submit themselves
if they want to live. And it becomes the more alien the more
specialized the division of labor becomes. Men do not live their own
lives but perform pre-established functions. While they work they
do not fulfill their own needs and faculties but work in alienation.[1]

Political characteristics

The middle-class portion of this group is very active
within the political realm and carries considerable influence. Their right to vote is not questioned or interfered
with. They are courted by politicians of all stripes, and
they share in the power and the decision-making structures. They have requested and consented to the pro-
tectorate-protector relationship between themselves and
the power apparatus of the community, state and nation.
The protectorate groups enter willingly into this relationship and consent to the reinforcing position of the
protector. They support and help guarantee the bases of
power on which the protector group is built.

One danger, however, is that in his continuous state of
heightened anxiety over the possibility of betraying the
culture, the individual in the threat-prone groups turns
more and more of his personal existence over to the
regulation of the state and more and more calls upon the
state for protection from the culture betrayers and from
himself. Marcuse has stated this in an interesting way:

The traditional borderlines between psychology on the one side and
political and social philosophy on the other have been made
obsolete by the condition of man in the present era: formerly
autonomous and identifiable psychical processes are being absorbed
by the function of the individual in the state—by his public
existence. Psychological problems therefore turn into political

---

[1] Marcuse, H. *Eros and civilization: A philosophical inquiry into Freud.* New
York: Vintage Books, The Beacon Press, 1962. p. 41.

problems; private disorder reflects more directly than before the disorder of the whole, and the cure of personal disorder depends more directly than before on the cure of the general disorder.[2]

Further Considerations

In a sense then, we might conclude that the threat-recoil cycle is linked with the reciprocal dissonance between the threatening and the threat-responder sectors. The turbulence created by their troubled exchanges reverberates throughout the community, creating a highly charged environmental condition. Within this tense relationship, there are two orders of problems that meet and clash.

One involves the individual in the threat-exciter group. A significant element of his problems appears to reside in his unacceptable behavior and life-style. This behavior is most frequently expressed in the external realm of an impoverished, deprived, disorganized and punitive environment; in the exile quality of his geographical habitat with the barriers and restrictions placed around it; in the lack of access to opportunity structures; in his exclusion from the privileges of the threat-avoidant group and isolation from any corporate body with community power; and also in his isolation from the major community channels through which he should be allowed to express his divergent life patterns.

The threat-receptive group, on the other hand, is more likely to be a victim of cultural tyranny. Its problems tend to interact with the internal problems of self-denial and self-punitiveness. Its members are more conceptually aware of their behavioral tendencies and desires that emphasize the cleavage between the life course of individuals and the

[2] *Ibid.*, p. xvii.

life course of the collective. Even where these behavioral tendencies may be species determined but culturally excluded, the threat-receptive group fails to reexamine the legitimacy or utility of each of these cultural taboos and instead attempts to renounce tabooed tendencies within themselves. This group is more likely to surrender its own control to the control of approved social structures.

We thus have two reciprocal orders of problems. On the one hand, there are the human problems that are related to cultural violations, environmental insult and inadequate cultural conditioning. On the other, there are the human problems of self-oppressions, which may, to an undetermined extent, be related to excessive cultural denials and conditioning. Both orders of human problems are crucial, and neither can be denied. Furthermore, since they antagonistically accentuate each other, it would seem reasonable to study and try to do something about both. Effective and efficient solutions may lie in simultaneous examination of the reciprocal interactions of both realms and the methods of moderating or ameliorating them together.

Reappraisal of Psychosocial Pathologies

Within the framework of the exciter-respondent type of analysis suggested above, there would be need for a total reexamination of many of the conditions of psychological and social pathology that are now treated as relatively independent disorders. Huge areas of such disorders as delinquency, mental retardation, mental illness and alcoholism would have to come in for this reappraisal. The reexamination would have particular bearing on the way in which we handle such problems and the types of mass solutions that we apply to them. It could lay the groundwork for a unified approach to human-behavior management in man-made environments. The reexamination would not necessarily invalidate all that we now believe or know about these separate conditions of pathology; rather it would be more deliberately tailored to the level of mass community action. It would provide a more unified basis for orchestrating the diverse behavioral agencies and systems, such as education, welfare, mental health and correction, that are now part of the social fabric.

The analysis of the exciter-reacter interaction suggests a major additional dimension or component of "pathology" – that psychosocial pathology is also a product of an exchange between exciter and responder, no matter what else it is. From an ecological perspective, this analysis would claim that pathology cannot properly be defined as existing only within the individual and his behavior. It is a psychosocial transformation that occurs in the confrontation between exciter and responder. Without inclusion of the responder term in the pathology equation, the divergent term is a partial and incomplete statement of the various psychosocial behavioral problems that are so troublesome to the community.

We should not begin with the assumption that divergence, discordance and pathology are the exclusive property of individuals. In the past we have borrowed the physiological analogue of disease controls as a means of looking at these problems and have dissected and analyzed all known properties of the organism in our avid search for their essence and cure. The basic point of departure has been the assumption of a flaw within the organism identified as the patient, client or subject. We have tried to translate these assumptions and findings into general applications.

If instead we can accept this refocused statement of the problem, we might begin to look at human psychosocial and behavioral problems as compounded from the exciter-responder exchanges. The exciter's unfamiliar and variant style of life or expression goads other members of the community into agitated internal and external responses; in other words, the style triggers a reciprocating emotive reaction from the community of responders. This reaction may contain mixtures of anxiety, danger, frustration or eroticism. Such relations then become part of the conditions of disturbance in the community. From an ecological point of view, mass efforts have to take these antipathetic interactions into consideration. Furthermore the exciter-responder analysis suggests that "pathology" or "disturbance" is a relative and shifting phenomenon, changing with various periods of time and with shifts in the psychosocial circumstances of communities. If there is a change in public concensus over which styles of life or behaviors are threatening, there will be a change in emphasis of community support for behavioral systems— the legal-correctional system may be emphasized at one time, the mental-health system at another, and education at still another.

3

The Psychological Protector
Apparatus of Society

The threat-recoil phenomenon is not only a mass expression of the stressed relationship between threat exciter and responder; it is also a force that moves and fuels the vast community apparatus that shapes, preserves and elaborates the culturally preferred traits and patterns of behavior, and protects the community against psychological threat. This apparatus involves two large elements of society, which, in varying degrees, moderate and referee the claims of individuals and society. One element, the power structure, will be reserved for later discussion. The other element is composed of the behavioral services of those social systems that help form and regulate the individual and the group according to socially preferred patterns of behavior and that moderate society to the needs of the individual. These community behavior-

47

regulator systems of society include social welfare, legal correction, education, mental health and, to a certain extent, religion.

The term "system" is used to describe something more than a community agency. Such systems as social welfare and legal correction are much more comprehensive and socially pervasive than the separate facilities of courts and detention centers, welfare agencies and school buildings, which are familiar fixtures in any community of the nation. They are a much more elaborate part of society, and as systems they encompass a vast, interrelated composite of 1) an ideology and philosophy about human ecology and human behavior, 2) bodies of knowledge, methods and technology related to this ideology and philosophy, 3) units or programs of training and knowledge generation (frequently part of university systems), 4) specific guild structures (professional associations), 5) an identifiable cadre of specialists who have been through the indoctrination and education of the system's training units and who have gone through the rites of passage associated with its guild structure and with society's sanction to practice the ideology and technology on its members, and 6) finally, and most important, its programs and operational delivery patterns, which are the delivery apparatus from the system to the individual, who is awarded by society to the system as its official client (seen most often in such facilities as courts, mental-health centers, school buildings, correctional institutions, and so forth).

The Behavior Regulators

The interlock of systems devoted to regulating community behavior has moved further and further toward the center of community life as the complexity of society has placed greater demands on the human organism. These systems operate within the gap between the semipermeable boundaries that separate the individual and the collective into related but discontinuous organisms. They operate like an artificial umbilical cord, providing an exchange system between the two and an access channel for social-cultural input into the human implant in the community.

Since the family by itself seems unable to accomplish the full range and scope of the coadaptation task that is required for community living in today's world, behavior-regulator systems such as legal correction, social welfare, medical/mental health and education have assumed increasing responsibility for this task. These artificial ecological management systems, therefore, are faced with the demand to become more functionally adept and more operationally sensitive to human requirements, while at the same time to become more productive facilitators of profitable contributions from man to the community.

Under the pressure of the threat-recoil cycles, however, the systems are diverted from reconstitution and enrichment of their creative roles. Instead they are deflected toward the task of providing a palliative to psychological threat and required to divert large proportions of their resources and energies for this purpose. The threat-avoidant population demands a proliferation of programs and operational patterns that can respond immediately to any hint of the threat of divergence. A bias is thus built into the systems that perverts them from their potential for increasing the capacity for growth within the individual and society. The ingenuity, inventiveness and effort that could be invested in designing operations for maximal development and for accentuating individual and community potential are frequently concentrated almost exclusively on the flaws and dwarfing aspects of man. The systems do not capitalize enough on human strengths and potential for advancement. It is as though the culture-bearing public is willing to settle for reducing threat and counteracting deviation and deficiency.

Focus on Behavior Management

This bias frequently takes a particular operational form. The most concrete and substantive aspect of human conditions to which people can react is behavior. It has visible dimensions and is immediately understandable; it is a palpable symbol that directly and concisely expresses a vast realm of an organism's life functioning. Under these circumstances, behavior takes precedence over all kinds of interactions that can do occur between the separate units of the individual regular systems' involvement with human life.

Under the influence of threat, the recoil process in the community brings pressure on the community-regulator systems to further narrow their focus and purpose. This narrowing consists of establishing higher priority for behavior control and revision than for behavior enhancement and construction. Thus the systems not only have a tendency to engage in a preoccupation with behavior as the most significant quality of human beings to which they will address many of their operations, but they even constrict their efforts further by an inordinate concentration on reconstruction and control of deviant or deficient behavior.

A large portion of the energies, resources and ingenuity of the systems of community regulation such as legal correction, social welfare, education and mental health are, as a consequence, syphoned off into mediation between the threatened population and these behaviors. Recurrent threat-recoil cycles have propagated innumerable behavior-control programs for delinquency, alcoholism, maladjustment and school deficiencies. The number and rate of development of such programs are beginning to clutter up the operations of the vast infrastructure of community-regulation agencies. Such programs become deeply embedded in the regulator systems and once brought to life, gain continued sustenance and maintenance. Their staffs invest themselves deeper and deeper in the specific problem behavior to which their program is dedicated. They gradually magnify the significance of this minute segment of human-behavior deviation until its control becomes of all-consuming importance to the general well-being of the society.

Management Functions of the Regulator Systems

The systems' behavior-control function is most directly affected by the threat-recoil cycles. The general functions served by the community-regulator systems, however, are much more inclusive, and their operations are much more complex. The system includes many subsystems and units that share the more general responsibility of regulating the engagements between individuals and communities. The systems are an integral part of the community lives; not only are they woven into the life of the human sectors, but they also have strong links with the political-power sectors and the economic sectors of local, state and federal structures. They become integral parts of government and emerge as government agencies.

In their larger tasks, the systems join ranks with the family to play various roles in binding the individual to the culture and in attempting to knit the life history of the individual and community into a single fabric. There are a number of such societal systems. In recent times, however the four that have had major responsibility for reinforcing the impact and control of the family on the behavior of the individual are the ones already mentioned: the educational, legal-correctional, social-welfare and mental-health systems.

These four systems will be the ones used as examples in this part of the book because they represent the current forms that have major behavior-regulating roles to play in this country. There are others rising on the horizon that promise to play increasingly significant roles in our lives, an example being the government-linked systems of housing and urban affairs. There is also another major institutionalized system that has an impact on adaptations of individuals to society and that is becoming more directly involved in the threat-recoil process — the system of religion. Although this system is of major importance in setting the standards of human behavior and life-styles in the society, it is not being used as an example in this chapter because of the deliberate separation of church and state in the United States. Thus it is not an integral part of the official psychological-protector apparatus of the society.

From the threat-recoil frame of reference, the four example systems form a legal and official coalition with the political-power structures that comes between the individual threat-exciter and larger threat-responder class of the community. When the threat-recoil cycle has reached proportions sufficient to activate the power structure, these systems are propelled into accelerated activities to control human behavior. From inside the community the vastness and intricacy of the systems mobilized during the cycles are not apparent. All that is visible is a simple community agency rendering services to individuals in need and calling on the community for increased support in cases of growing threat. The system of which the agency is a part, however, is enormously complex and widely ramified throughout the fabric of society.

In order to grasp more clearly the total system concept and to understand the way in which its components are related, a brief description of each component follows.

Constituent Parts of a Regulator System

Ideology

Each system has its own ideology, which is composed of a basic philosophical approach to humans and their problems. It includes a set of assumptions about human behavior, a group of theories and an elaborate body of working hypotheses. The ideology is a broad, generalized orientation toward the nature/nurture relationship of human beings to their environments. It may, for instance, be based on a philosophy that views the human organism as a bundle of potential capacities, skills, abilities, etc., that can be realized through certain carefully constructed conditions and circumstances being brought to bear on the organism from outside. This might be one way of roughly characterizing the educational orientation.

Another orientation and set of assumptions may look upon the human organism as basically biological, with certain capacities from growth and decline, well-being and pathology. This brief statement may be used as a suggestion of the medical/mental-health orientation.

From another point of view, human nature may be conceived of as random instances of chance assignment to either a generous or a depriving environment, either culturally and economically advantaged or disadvantaged. This assumption would not be incompatible with the ideology of social welfare.

Another recognizable orientation is that which is framed in a good/bad dimension of human nature. The assumption within this orientation is either that human nature is essentially bad and that monitoring networks must be maintained to control this tendency; or, within this same orientation, that man is inherently good and must be fostered in this direction and protected from outside contamination. This is somewhat akin to the religious frame of reference.

Each of these orientations is characterized by elaborate collections of assumptions about human nature and human behavior. Extensive theories, collections of information and detailed data and conclusions about human behavior have been derived and developed from these assumptions.

Methods and technology

Each system has developed specific methods and strategies for shaping, changing, controlling and regulating human conduct within the societal context. The methods are directly related to and derived from the ideology. The system of education, for instance, has various methods and techniques of teaching. The social-welfare system has various methods of casework. The legal-correctional system has various methods of trial, law enforcement, punishment and probation. The mental-health system has various forms of psychotherapy, shock and psychosurgery. The systems' techniques are the delivery accesses through which the total institutional impact of the systems is delivered to individuals. The methods and techniques are the keystones to the operational patterns of the systems and the functional binding of ideology, knowledge and assumptions into direct action on individual-societal accommodations. In addition, the techniques are a major test of the social utility of the systems.

It is at the level of technology that extensive changes are made possible in the processes and results of the reciprocity between individual and community. Through the changes are accomplished major effects on human behavior and patterns of life. At the systems' present stage of development, this technology is relatively imprecise and inexact. It is only recently that the scientific method has begun to have an across-the-board influence on the technology of any one system. With the increase in the effectiveness of the systems' behavior-shaping and behavior-regulating technology, there is an ever-increasing need to consider how to use the systems and for what ends. There is a growing and impelling need for the developed society to look to what it is about in relationship to regulation of human behavior. In fact, as indicated in the introductory chapter of this book, there is already a crisis in the relationship between individuals and societies. As we gain greater technological and scientific control over human behavior, this crisis will be intensified, and we will have to search deeply for a reconceptualization of this relationship.

Training and knowledge-generating units

More and more the community-regulator systems are locating their training and knowledge-generating components in the university and college. The specialists who assume training and knowledge-generating functions in the system become very influential in the guilds of the systems and in the types of operational-delivery systems that are developed in the community. They are the selectors and the molders of the workers in the system; they develop the primary rites of passage that turn the individual into a system specialist.

Specialists and their guilds

The corps of working specialists, so trained, becomes a professional group that has acquired the ideology, body of knowledge and technology of the system. Such specialists belong to strong professional guilds with highly developed vested interests in the system and its operational patterns. The guilds look to the pattern to translate functionally the ideology and technology of their system into community structures and action; these organizational patterns mirror the governing structures of the society. As an example, the educational system has local, state, regional and national professional associations that foster and champion the interests of their specialist corps. Very frequently, as in the case of the medical, educational and social-work guilds, they even develop legislative and other government lobbies to enhance and protect the interests and contributions of the operational patterns and programs in their own systems.

Each guild has developed means of controlling its members and holding them to a particular code and set of standards. The guilds differ in the status given them by society, and this status affects not only their relationship to the community and national power and government echelons but also their ability to influence decision making at the upper levels of the power structure and to obtain funds and authority to translate their ideology and knowledge into the management and development of human behavior. The current status of a guild determines whether it is likely to be called on at the height of a threat-recoil cycle and which operational pattern will be given prominence in the process of mobilization and deployment of national, state and local resources to deal with the threat. The status at that time also influences the kind of interpretation that will be given the psychologically threatening behavior.

The guilds are not only rooted in the operational pattern that is staffed and administered by their specialists, but they are also firmly rooted in the university system. The university feeds both guilds and the operational patterns by acting as the depository of its ideology, the generator of new theories, knowledge and technology, and also the training center for continuous replacement of the specialist.

Operational patterns

Each system that becomes institutionalized in the social fabric of the community has specific operational-delivery patterns that are the hallmark of the system. It is the operational pattern through which the specialists of the system deliver the ideology, technology and power to the point of intersection between individuals and the social structures. In relationship to the threat-recoil cycles, the operational patterns of the systems are maneuvered between the threat exciter and the threat responder when mass emotive responses reach national levels.

The patterns take the form of human-service agencies at local, state, regional and national levels. They are the action instruments of the systems and the most crucial element of the systems because they agglutinate the ideology, technology and specialists into a single organizational component with the capability of inducting, processing and discharging individuals who are awarded to their jurisdiction. This jurisdictional authority is one of the most important characteristics of the operational pattern and the system to which it is related. It represents mandates from the community that transfer social power to the operational pattern. Some of these mandates are law, for example, welfare authority in adoption or state-mental-hospital authority over committed patients. Some of them are contractual agreements between government and agency. In addition, the specialists within the operational pattern are usually empowered to practice the behavior-shaping and regulating techniques of their system on fellow citizens through such community sanctions as licensing, certification and merit-system ratings.

Each system has its own characteristic form of operational pattern to shape and regulate community behavior. Education has schools; social welfare has welfare agencies and family-services agencies; legal correction has courts, detention centers and training schools; mental health has clinics and hospitals. Each system relies on its characteristic operational pattern to solve problems of individual threat to the community. When the agitation of the threat responders reaches the power structure and that structure engages the system, the immediate reaction of the system is to deploy its traditional operational patterns or to request authority to build replicas of the same model. No matter what the substantive nature of the threat, the system relies on its conventional and classical operational pattern. It rarely designs a special type of operational pattern to fit the problem, but usually focuses the problems to fit its existing pattern.

Depending on which system is called upon by the power structure at the height of the cycle, however, the same threatening behavior can have quite different operational patterns applied to it. In the case of delinquency, for instance, the medical/mental-health system will offer the clinic or even a psychiatric hospital as the solution. If education is called upon, it will offer a special school program; if the legal-correction system is activated, it will offer juvenile courts, training schools and detention centers.

Entry points, interventions and goals

Each system has 1) its characteristic entry point into the threatening behavior or life pattern, 2) its characteristic interventions, and 3) its characteristic goals in relationship to changing the individual producers of threat.

The entry point of the mental-health and educational systems is into interpersonal and intra-personal components of the individual producing the psychological threat. The entry point of the social-welfare system is the environmental circumstances surrounding the individual and the setting of his behavior. The legal-correction system concentrates primarily on the specific threatening behavior and its divergence from particular behavioral-cultural codes.

Each system also has its characteristic form of intervention. For education it is teaching, for mental health therapy, for social welfare aid and support, for legal correction direct authority and physical control.

Furthermore, the system has a characteristic goal when it engages the threat. The educational system's major goal is meliorating or inducing positive change and development of the individual. In a sense, it seeks to construct behaviors or life patterns that minimize psychological threat. The characteristic tool of the mental-health system is restoration or reconstruction of the individual and his behavior. The primary goal of the social-welfare system is to improve the environing circumstances or reconstruct the setting of the behavior. The goal of the legal-correction system in relationship to threat is to constrain the behavior or the individual producing the behavior.

The characteristic entry points, interventions and goals will be discussed in greater detail in the chapter on operational patterns.

Definitional Recapitulation

Let us review the material that has been covered in discussing the systems. In the relationships between the threat-exciter class and the threat-responder class, there are special societal systems that join in a coalition with the political-power structures to mediate between them. These are the same systems that have general responsibility for stimulating mutual growth and accommodations between the individual and society. In the threat-recoil process, they are pulled in the direction of behavior correction and behavior regulation in conformity to the culture's proscriptions. Using this frame of reference, we might define the behavior-shaping and behavior-regulating programs and operational patterns of the community-regulator systems as an aggregate or composite of ideology, technology, specialists and specialist guilds, and components of universities.

The Systems and the Threat-Recoil Process

The systems have an essential role in the segmented relationships and transactions that take place during the threat-recoil process. One or the other of them shares the spotlight with the threat exciter during the heat of controversy. As the sense of crisis mounts, both the community of threat responders and the power structures turn toward the systems. Legislation is passed that nominates one or the other of the community-regulator systems to intervene in the tense situation. They are given access to increased funds and supplied with the means for mobilizing their operational patterns, for stepping up the level of their research, and for training increasing numbers of their specialists.

There is a certain capriciousness in the choice of the system to alleviate social distress and curb threatening behavior. These choices, however, can be traced to such things as the current prominence of the system and the professionals attached to it and also can be correlated with the same resources as are replenished when the community is threatened. The system chosen is usually one that has a rich storehouse of resources, is vigorously adding to the number of its specialists, increasing the strength of the schools or departments that train them, accelerating its research activities, building its operational patterns, and making public pronouncements on the nature of the threat and methods of dealing with it.

The focus of these recurrent tides of threat and recoil changes from year to year, and with the changing focus we can observe the emphasis of the systems shifting with it. Part of this, of course, is the natural riveting of professional attention on current issues. There is also, however, the realistic factor of money flowing more freely toward those areas that are causing the greatest current distress to communities.

4

The Politics of
Behavior Regulation

The larger function served by the major community
behavior-regulator systems was conceptualized in the
preceding chapter as reciprocity and growth enhancement
between individual and community. The specific function
in relationship to the threat-recoil phenomenon was
described as behavior mediation in conflicts between the
claims and rights of individuals and communities. In this
chapter the contention will be made that these purposes
are sometimes obscured and adulterated by purposes that
grow out of 1) the systems' structural ties to political-
power processes and professional guilds, and 2) the basic
power dynamics of the human beings who manage the
systems. It is not possible to measure the extent to which
these two considerations dilute the growth and mediation
aims of the systems and their operating units. Our

discussion will look at some of the factors and content of such dilutions. It will also sketch the way in which a system's maintenance frequently assumes functional autonomy, independent of the goal of preventing or repairing cleavages between the individual and society. It will point out personality power dynamics that seem to conflict with the systems' human-service aims.

Adulteration of Purpose

Mayors, governors and presidents have run on platforms that aim at full mobilization against these psychological threats, for example, a separate mental-health department, a special program of prisons and corrections, an attack on crime and delinquency. Powerful administrative programs are set up to combat them. State and federal legislators have built reputations and careers designing legislation associated with threat and recoil. The judicial branch of government has expended considerable effort and concern in handing down new interpretations of existing legislation and redefining or reviving old rulings bearing on the process. Powerful coalitions and partnerships have been forged between governing groups and agencies around the issues raised by the threat exciters and threat responders. The link between government and the behavior-shaping and behavior-regulating functions of the major regulator systems has become so close that the governing executive is frequently identified by the public as the executor of the actions of a system. Conversely, the operations of the systems may be described as being oriented as much toward psychopolitical as human-service considerations in their execution.

Most universal operational patterns have direct and indirect lines of authority leading to the governing structures of city, county, state and nation. Those that do not have hierarchical administrative ties are frequently the benefactors, directly or indirectly, of official public funds. In fact, an operational unit is not likely to survive and endure unless it is buttressed with money that has become a regular item in the annual budget of the governing body of its geographical jurisdiction.

Out of these reality factors has come the necessity for continual accommodations between power and human-care concerns. Although these are not necessarily antithetical, they are frequently divergent. A constant requirement of our human condition is that these two sets of concerns should find common directions and that there be constant alert and attention to the danger of divergence.

One possibility of divergence lies in the political atmosphere itself. The professionals who direct the systems' operational units must perform their duties within this atmosphere and must constantly negotiate with the political figures who are dominant within their jurisdictions. Ideally, the directors should have the capacity not only to subsume the concerns, conceptions and needs of the socially estranged populations that make up their constituency, but they should also have the capacity to understand the motives and mechanics of the power-oriented political figures. The ability to subsume the construction and nature of both the discordants and the dominant political leaders is a rare and ephemeral talent that seldom coexists in the same individual; and yet, this is one of the most crucial human capacities required by our times. It is very difficult to maintain both orientations because the executives and executive staffs of the operational units grow away from the taproots of their human-service drives and specialties as they strengthen their taproots in the political soil. All of the elements are weighted in the direction of political accommodation and performance. Their major exchanges are with political figures, and their major responses are to the political climate and its various groups interacting within the power frame of reference. Since much of the science and art of politics has to do with the assimilation, manipulation and distribution of power, it is natural that the operational-unit executives would become immersed in this process and begin to develop those skills, drives and tendencies that will equip them to be power figures.

The very real political linkages of the systems' operational units to various governing structures place the operational units directly in the legislative, judicial and executive mainstream of government, with the most basic tie to the current administration of governing bodies. There is a direct-line relationship between education, welfare, mental health, etc., and the current administration in government office at national, state and local levels. The executive and supervisory staffs of the systems' operational patterns are therefore directly lodged in the power orbit and subject to the directional forces of the political-power field. They are also the liaison between the professional guilds and the administration. They are the interlocutors who interpret the political currents of their guilds to government power figures and the political currents of government to the guilds. In terms of the most direct, insistent and controlling pressures, then, the professional executives are subjected to the needs and concerns of both the political-power elements of government and the political-power elements of their guilds. It is quite conceivable that their roles and day-to-day operations would become more and more embedded in this complex of impelling political considerations and necessities.

One could imagine that without the daily visibility of the personal suffering of their socially estranged constituency and without the human interchange of feeling and negotiation, the figure of the troubled and threatening individual would become dim and unreal. His suffering and his turbulence would seem more symbolic than actual, more peripheral than central. Furthermore, the estranged and threatening individual is to a very large extent a socially powerless individual. When we discuss such culturally discordant conditions and behaviors as mental illness, delinquency, sexual deviation and alcoholism, we are not only describing the estranged class; we are also talking about relatively powerless groups that have the weight of the community arrayed against them. This does not mean that this weight is always used, or that it is necessarily used in negative ways against them; but it does say that the balance of power is against them. The concordant majority has the whole panoply of socioeconomic, political and psychological power at its disposal. Thus it is very difficult for those human-service specialists who become conversant with power, learn the language of political transaction, and achieve skill in transactions of diplomacy and statemanship to maintain a perspective that incorporates both the powerless and the powerful.

Competition for Resources

There are a number of community behavior-regulator systems operating in the political orbit. The paraphernalia of each includes many agencies with mandates to deal with the community's human problems. This elaborate operational apparatus must be maintained if a system is to compete with other systems devoted to personal-societal problems. When a new form of human-societal threat begins to ascend above the threshold of concern and become a domestic crisis, the political structures and power structures move into their protector roles and start to mobilize national, state or local resources. An administrative plan for crises resolution is drawn up and put forward; legislative acts are passed; appropriations are made. In such a field of forces, each system and its operational patterns must also mobilize. Each guild marshals its own authority, and its chief professionals advise and consult the legislator and the executive about the community problem. Each has a solution. They begin to compete for leadership of and responsibility for the major thrust against the threat and for the programs and funds the authorities are making available. Since many threats are recurrent, the systems gradually build up a vast collection of programs and operating patterns. The executive staff must devote constantly increasing attention and energy to competition with other organizations to maintain this extensive paraphernalia. All of this contributes to increasing concerns with power relationships and responsibilities.

One can observe the competition for public support and political support at state, local and national levels. The education department competes with the welfare department, the mental-health department makes its claim for funds, and so forth. Any time a new problem behavior or human condition captures the public imagination and raises its level of anxiety, each system vigorously argues its claim to deal with the problem. When the problem of mental retardation or juvenile delinquency looms large on the social scene, for instance, we can see each system strengthening that part of its characteristic operational pattern devoted to these particular problems. The executives in the upper echelon of the systems' operational areas alert their guilds to the imminent legislation. The guilds in turn build and present their claims to the area. Because any one of these human problems is so intermeshed with the other, it is quite possible for more than one system to present a good case for its responsibilities and authority in the area. In the field of mental retardation, for example, legitimate cases can be made by public welfare, education or medicine. Since all of these systems have operational patterns firmly anchored in communities, it is quite possible for them to point to these concrete structures as possible defenses and stations of community and individual aid.

As an example of the competiveness among the guilds, a recent piece of legislation was passed requiring a massive study of the extent of a childhood problem, the existing resources and the operational solutions that might be expanded across the board. The system chosen in the legislative act to give advice on the granting of the money to conduct the study informed its own professional guild. This guild immediately incorporated a group of professional associations, with dominating representation from its own guild, to apply for the grant. Then there ensued a series of contests, maneuvers, position statements and political operations among the various invested guilds that could be compared to a political election or a corporate struggle. The point being made here is not that this type of competition among systems and guilds is necessarily harmful. It is probably very fortunate that a single system does not dominate the individual-societal problem field. In this way it is possible for varying approaches and systems to be applied. The point is, however, that the executive staffs in the upper hierarchy of the systems' operational arms must give a considerable amount of their time and capacity to such real considerations. Furthermore, there is always the danger of distorting the systems in the direction of power and competition at the expense of advocacy of and care for the needs of their estranged constituency.

Upward Mobility in the Organization.

The necessity for the professional to function in the political-power arena has a particular influence on the systems' internal dynamics and their operating organizations. One of the considerations that influences successful upward mobility within the systems and their operational units is skill in political, diplomatic and power functioning. This in itself is a realistic factor in any area of human existence in social systems. In the human-care professions, however, it has a diluting effect on care and service motivations. It is very difficult to argue this point, and our research techniques and knowledge of organizational behavior cannot present evidence on the point; it seems reasonable, however, to hypothesize that the emphasis on these skills and motivations is antithetical to the crucial needs of the estranged populations. In fact, it may be argued that this type of orientation, if institutionalized, pulls human-care specialists away from their constituency and encourages the same rejecting attitude within them that exists within the threatened public.

If it is true as suggested here that even within the systems the pull is toward entrenched cultural groups, there would seem to be a powerful tendency for the culturally estranged individual to be abandoned even by the caretaker. The systems' operational arms would be continually attracted toward the power groups and their interests. The weight of the systems' efforts would be subtly conditioned to responsiveness to these power interests, and an advocacy in behalf of the interests and needs of the cultural alien would be slowly extinguished or submerged. Through time the power-holding segment of society would become their reference group. This tendency for professionals to turn away from their constituencies is understandable if one takes into consideration the attitude of the general society toward anyone who is associated with the threatening populations. There is such a socially negative quality about these denigrated groups that even those who work with them become suspect and undesirable. As the taboo associated with the cultural alien spreads to encompass those who would show active compassion for him, the champions themselves undergo the rites of alienation.

Guild Concern

Another deflection from the expressions of care for the estranged populations is the systems' tendency to orient themselves toward their professional guilds. Considerable energy is expended in guild concerns and operations involving protection of their vested interests and in competitive maneuvers and operations aimed toward other professional guilds performing in the same arenas. In the daily functioning of any operational pattern one encounters many examples of the abrasions and the barriers to trust and openness created by guild competitiveness. It is quite understandable, however, that professionals should cling to their reference groups. The suspiciousness among professional cultures is no different from the competitive and separatist tendencies of any distinguishable social group. The staking of claims to a territory and the fierce defense of this territory are exemplified in the behaviors of lowest to the highest animals. Encroachment of one group on the turf claimed by another will almost always bring retaliation. Therefore the fact that this human principle should operate in professionals as well as in any other human collective should not be surprising. When you add to this the fact that the guilds are not only the sources of professional identity but also the sanctioning cores for ideology about human behavior, and technology for intervention and mediation, as well as the providers of ties to the professional-opportunity structures and community-power structures, then the amount of jealousy and hours of time used for this purpose are even more understandable.

Such guild concerns, however, do detract from the systems' missions and their operational patterns. Programs must be distorted in order to accommodate competitive guild concerns. One has to be sure that there is a social worker, or a psychologist, or a pediatrician on the staff, not because these skills or orientations are necessary to the task or the target, but merely to accommodate vested interests. A proposal for a problem solution is examined not only in light of the aim or nature of the problem, but in light of inclusion of all professionals who may feel that guild needs should be represented. It is not unusual for trading operations to be conducted between professionals who are designing research projects or programs. In order to gain acceptance of his guild's point of view, the professional will make concessions to the point of view of others. Again, this is not because his best judgment dictates such a move, but because of expediency.

Such trading or competitiveness is not always in operation or necessarily the focus of concern or activities. Furthermore, many professionals recognize their own tendencies in this direction and are conscious of the web of involvement with their own professional reference groups. Many of them would willingly renounce such ties if they could find ways of being socially productive without the aids and supports of their vested groups. Nevertheless, these guild factors remain a detracting and diluting addition to the price that the professional must pay in the power marketplace. This summation reduces the total reserve that is available to the discordant, threatening and alienated groups that are his constituents. The professional who, on the other hand, is empathically related to his alienated charges always runs the risk of neglecting his guild support. Such exclusion leaves him in a position of isolation from the mainstreams of both his professional guild and its entry points into power structures. His ideas are not likely to get a hearing, and his efforts with and in behalf of the estranged groups are less likely to gain support or sanction.

There is a further negative aspect of guild concerns and competition. The professionals become so conceptually ensnared in their trademark patterns and agencies that they cannot see the problem itself clearly and directly. Their characteristic and traditional structures become such a symbol of their guilds, such an image-making trademark, that they cannot depart from them and use their imagination, theories and knowledge to invent and create new processes or machinery for problem resolution. They are so glued to their traditional structures, such as schools and clinics, that any new human problem presented to them is immediately viewed through such structures. The problem is twisted to fit the structural pattern, rather than a pattern or new solution being shaped to the measures of the problem.

The question that these facts raise is not whether we can put a stop to guild concerns. This is not possible and may not even be desirable. Rather the question is to what extent are these concerns now intruding on the systems' major human missions and tasks. How many of these operations can be tolerated before the systems and their operational patterns become functionally autonomous, diverting the major part of their energies into power concerns and guild concerns and leaving the basic human problems relatively untouched?

Ascension in the Hierarchy of the Systems

Another factor, in addition to power concerns, militates against a deep and abiding contract with the estranged or threat-inducing minorities toward whom the agencies are supposed to be oriented. The individuals who have the greatest capacity for conceptualizing and developing systematic ideas about human life and behavior are more likely to be attracted away from deep and long-term immersion into the lives of the estranged minorities and into the upper hierarchies of the behavior-regulator systems. Such individuals, because of this capacity, not only find themselves in top executive and supervisory levels of the systems' operational arms, but also gravitate toward the semicloistered enclaves of the university. Here they conceptualize the lives and problems of the estranged minorities from a distance. The training that the university-based faculty gives the students who are preparing to staff the systems suffers the anemia of the conceptializers' removed position. Because they are not participant conceptualizers, their facts about encounter with and immersion into the phenomenon are many times removed. The theories that guide our systems and the training that shapes their staffs is therefore rarely derived directly from the phenomenon.

Recent sociological literature has indicated the change that takes place in the picture of the problems and their dimensions when there is direct participation in the phenomenon. The view of the scientist who participates in the lives of patients in state mental hospitals, prisoners in prison, or slum dwellers in seething Negro, Puerto Rican and Mexican slums takes on aspects and dimensions that are quite different from the theories and pictures offered by university nonparticipants.

The Threat Provoker and the Professional Caretaker

On the other hand, front-line specialists who do participate in the lives of their constituency often exist in a symbiotic relationship with threatening individuals of the community. Policemen, psychotherapists, social workers, or ministers may all enter into deep and intensive exchanges of themselves with their constituents. Such a psychological intercourse between two human beings has profound transfer effects that have never really been captured in the theories of human relationship. No matter how the professional would like to think about his continuous encounter with the discordant or threatening individual, one conclusion seems to be valid. After they have experienced intense exposure to each other, the barrier separating professional and discordant into two kinds of people begins to become permeable and pliable. The professional interceding agent, if he is to be effective in his role, must be able to project himself into the position of his constituent; it is through this projection that, he comes to know the other end of the reciprocal human exchange. The recipient client is subsumed within the experience of the interceder in ways that can have immeasurable consequences.

Some of these consequences are very dramatic. In the early days of street-corner programs, some of the gang workers became intensely engrossed with their delinquent charges. Their involvement was so complete that they deflected their goals and reference away from the central-community agency that employed them and cast their sympathy with the gangs. Another type of reciprocal experience is found over and over again in the psychotherapy clinic. The intense exchange between psychotherapist and client, particularly if the therapist truly risks himself in a human encounter, can be intense and profound. The influence is bidirectional. There is a compelling intensity and satisfaction in such an exchange that is rarely experienced in everyday human relationships. For example, there can be a stirring loss of self within self, like the experience of love. The terms "transference" and "countertransference" cannot begin to capture the meaning of it. With it can come a subtle loosening of the bonds that hold the psychotherapist to his culture and its taboos and even to the cognitive categories provided him by his discipline. He becomes a man who is, to an extent, free of the limits of his culture and outside the limiting boundaries of his profession. He is a man and knows he is a man exactly like the discordants to whom he contracts himself. He looks out across the arc between himself and his opposite and sees himself on the other side. In this merged picture of discordant and interceding agent, the shades of difference between them are blurred. If the professional turns back and gazes at the distant agency to which he is attached, he sees only the upward vertical chain of the agency hierarchy to the power hierarchy. Such a vista appears to be only a faint structure that has little to do with what he is. Both the alarm of the community members and the social-control concerns of the power segments become a faint, distant sound, intruding only vaguely on the sense of an intense and important human confrontation.

These front-line workers in the community behavior-regulator systems are very crucial and precious agents of society. They are the humanizing substance of society, the communicators between what is human and important in the nature of individuals and the psychological condition-ing techniques of the regulator systems that shape individuals in social and cultural directions. Without these mediators the individual would be relatively defenseless against the organized power of society, and the operational patterns of the regulator systems would be in danger of allying themselves completely with the power forces of society. Such a danger seemed to be realized in Nazi-dominated Germany. The community behavior-regulator systems were completely diverted to power. Professional scientism within these systems took on extremely destructive expressions like the attempted extermination of the mentally ill. The ever-present danger of such abuses resides in the existing and logical alliance between governing bodies and community-regulator systems, between power-driven leaders and social structures. The linking agent, the front-line worker in the system, is a modulator between social oppression and human expression. Ways should be invented to strengthen his position and provide him with sanction and support for his task.

The Power-Succorance Issue

In the perhaps exaggerated contrast between the upper hierarchy of policy makers and decision-making personnel in the systems and the personnel directly in contact with the systems' constituents, other crucial aspects of the power issue present themselves. These aspects are concerned with ways in which checks can be brought on systems to reorient them to the advocacy role assumed by the front-line specialists. Such specialists lack influence in the major policy decisions of the systems. Their direct knowledge of and penetration into the concerns, culture and ethos of the systems' constituents is not effectively integrated into the operations of the systems. Because they form the synapses for the outer reaches of the systems and the alienated populations, they could provide a crucial transceiver function that would make the systems and their operational delivery patterns true interlocutors between the needs and claims of the alienated groups and the general society. Some of the rigidities of the operational-delivery patterns and some of their obvious failures in acculturating and modulating society to human requirements can conceivably lie in the front-line specialists' lack of decision-shaping influence.

This inequity in the systems' power and succorance operations also robs the society of a feedback mechanism that could keep it growing and changing. It closes one of the possibilities of further knowledge of its own humanness, further understanding of the nature of man. It causes the systems to become bulwarks against self-disclosure and protectors of the status quo, preventing society from measuring the beliefs and folktales that dictate patterns of human behavior against the realities of human nature. It closes off an important avenue for periodic refurbishing of the cultural content and for relinquishing old repressive customs that no longer serve a useful social purpose. Much more than this, it may be responsible for encouraging the systems' functional autonomy and operational-delivery patterns. It could encourage the continued existence and growth of massive programs and processes within the systems that serve no useful problem-solving function, but that go on perpetuating and proliferating programs and processes because they have the appearance of protecting the general public against all types and varieties of threat. It could lead to systematic self-indulgence with no way of checking on the systems' efficiency of social effectiveness.

Summary

The central focus of this book is the particular coloring that psychological threat and recoil give human affairs in the community and the specialized influence that this process has on the community behavior-regulator systems. The regulator systems form the connections between individuals and the society. They are as crucial for the existence and growth of both the individual and the collective as is the umbilical cord that plays such a vital role in the relationship between the embryo and its maternal host. Through this linkage network in the living community the individual and society are formed and re-formed to reflect and reciprocate each other. Through it they can be guaranteed a creative coexistence.

The community regulator systems were defined as a composite of 1) ideology and philosophy about human ecology and human behavior, 2) bodies of knowledge, methods and technology related to this ideology and philosophy, 3) units or programs of training and knowledge generation that are usually part of university systems, 4) specific guild structures, 5) a cadre of specialists indoctrinated in its ideology and technology, and 6) a collection of facilities or operational-delivery arm of its ideology, knowledge and technology. Under the influence of the threat-recoil process, the regulator systems are being gradually transformed into behavior-control systems, with the overt behavior of human beings receiving primary attention. The strong influence of psychological threat on this network and the haphazard and unregulated nature of the tides of threat and recoil that continually sweep across the community, state and nation leave a further indelible impression on the network, including both a predominance of programs devoted to controlling and reforming culturally divergent behavior and an adulteration of the network's creative and constructive functions.

The interlace of community-regulator systems supports the family in its social-personal task. It functions at the point of creative stress between individuals and collective forms, capitalizes on the discontinuities between the two units for the growth and enhancement of both, and mediates individual claims against social claims. Systems such as education, social welfare, legal correction and mental health constitute this interlace. There is, however, a danger within the regulator systems of strengthening the executive function that is concerned with social power and control over the front-line operations concerned with the rights of individuals as they are exemplified in the rejected populations of society. The quality of psychocultural threat encourages the alliance of human-care programs with power structures and power motivations. This alliance further weakens the precarious social position of the estranged groups and makes them vulnerable to scapegoating and to displacement of psychocultural conflicts in the personality of the threatened individuals.

5

The Operational Patterns

The Operational-Delivery Apparatus of the Behavior-Regulator Systems

The operational patterns of the behavior-regulator systems are the final pathway for operational delivery from the various elements of the behavior-regulator system to the interlock between individual and society. These elements include the philosophy, body of knowledge, professional corps and special technology of the system. The operational-delivery apparatus is generally dominated by its procedures of methods. These specialized techniques usually determine the organizational structure, form and administration of the operational pattern and give it its distinctive identity. The methods or techniques are in turn derived from the system's philosophy and accumulating body of knowledge. The technique of teaching, for

81

instance, shapes the schools; the technique of psychotherapy shapes the clinics, and so forth.

The operational pattern is also to some extent the legitimized delivery apparatus for the collective power of society. This power is delivered through the apparatus to the individual in an attempt to harmonize his processes with those of the community. It is expressed in legislative authority to the agency or operational pattern and in licensing or certification of its professional staff, plus popular support for the use of the particular institutional intervention into the lives of individuals. As this power is expressed in current operational patterns, it is brought to bear on individuals to cause them to organize their impulses, forces and behaviors in ways that are compatible with collective living. This appears to be the case whether the operational pattern is a corrective institution, school or mental-health institution. In each case, the legitimate forces of society join with the philosophy and techniques of the behavior-regulator systems to nudge the individual into socially determined directions.

Classes of Operational Patterns

Political Link versus Political Separation

We can distinguish between behavior-regulator systems that are directly linked to the state and usually supported by it and those that maintain a clear separation from the state and exist primarily on independent support. These systems' operational patterns can be divided into the same general groups. The first group of patterns is an integral part of the significant tripartite constellation of behavior-shaping, economic and formal power structures. As state-controlled and state-financed patterns, they are subject to all the economic and power maneuvers, vicissitudes and strategies that are involved in state machinery, with all the attendant manipulability, vulnerability and established communication channels. In any effort to influence human behavior through operational patterns in this group, the leverage points are easy to grasp and maneuver. Any move toward change can be funneled through a pyramidal power hierarchy in which the channels and authorities are clearly drawn. Welfare departments, probation programs and mental-health departments are examples. In a democratic society, the second group, the nonpolitical or private behavior-shaping patterns, is not directly linked to state and therefore not as easily accessible to cultural concensus and public pressure. Examples of these are the church in the regulator system of religion, and private agencies in social-welfare-regulator systems.

Nurturant versus Emergency Patterns

The operational patterns of the behavior-regulator systems have two different types of functions. Both try to make events in the lives of individuals and in the lives of communities as compatible as possible and to integrate these into an orderly interactive process; both types bind individual to community. But one has sustained responsibility for all individuals over a long period of time, while the other operates only episodically in response to alarm and on selected groups of individuals whose behavior evokes upset in the community. The first might be thought of as nurturant patterns, while the second has the character of emergency-care patterns.

The nurturant patterns

These constitute the patterns of the regulator system that assume long-term, sequence-binding, universal responsibility for each community inhabitant. They shape and regulate human behavior, as do all the patterns; but in addition they attempt to weave the experiential units resulting from exchange between environment and individual into a unified human chronology. The patterns most typically involved are school and church, and the systems to which they belong are education and religion. Because of their sequence-linking responsibility for unfolding each individual life and because of their constant and long-term coupling with individuals, they have a profound and long-lasting influence on human development and behavior fields.

Nurturant operational patterns are the basic civilizing agencies of society. Their primary task is to modulate the growth and development of individuals according to the requirements of living and functioning in social groups and established environments. In order to be effective civilizing instruments they must devote major attention and effort to long-term human-instinct conversion and the compatible balancing of individual drives with community restraints and requirements. They must also create and maintain channels of reciprocity between individuals and community units. If they stray too far in directions that favor either the individual or society, they could foster incompatibility between the two.

Among the regulator patterns that have sustained responsibility for harmonizing individuals and communities, the nurturant pattern of school is the only one that is formally linked to government structures and political power. It is interesting that this is the pattern most subject to increasing public criticism and attack. The overt reasons are quite varied and frequently contradictory, sometimes seeming vague and irrational. The on-slaught comes from many different groups and directions. There seems to be an increase in both the velocity and the frequency of waves of assault on the schools in spite of increased community financial backing and support for the schools' authority over future generations.

The emergency-care patterns

These patterns are largely correcting and control patterns. Their responsibility is episodic and directed at the lives only of selected community members whose behavior arouses alarm in others. This type pattern consists of a group of human services and agencies that back up the nurturant apparatus. The multivaried patterns that bear such emergency and episodic responsibility are numerous. In general, they fall within the systems of legal correction, social welfare, and medical/mental health. For example, the restorative patterns of psychopolitical systems, such as psychiatric clinics, family-service agencies and guidance centers, are likely to serve emergency functions for the community and the individual. The same is true of coercive and containment patterns, such as detention centers, probation programs, training schools and jails.

When there is a signal of psychosocial alarm in the community, these patterns are quickly moved to intervene between community concern and the episodic behaviors that have triggered such alarm. They therefore constitute the emergency task force of the community. They concentrate mainly on a group of residual behavioral patterns that have escaped the influence of the nurturant patterns, and their clientele usually represents failures of the nurturant group to harmonize the individual and the community. The accelerated spread of emergency patterns may reflect the increasing frequency of instances of dissociations between individuals and communities, or it may be interpreted as a result of the growing inadequacy of nurturant community structures to engage man and society in meaningful and mutually supportive exchanges.

Fixed and Fluid Patterns

Facility Bound

So far we have viewed behavior-shaping or life-influencing patterns and programs in terms of their linkage or lack of ties to political bodies. We have divided them according to the span and duration of their control over individual lives. Now we will explore another organizational or agency dimension that involves the extent to which the operational patterns and programs are tied to fixed institutional structures or operate free of fixed structures in the open community.

In the fixed patterns, the methods and the facility are inextricably wedded; hospitals, schools, clinics and prisons are examples. For such patterns there are very standard and traditional housings, built according to a blueprint. Society rarely thinks of the elements of the operational pattern and the structure as being independent and separable. Structure and method always appear together. The function of education or teaching, for example, is rarely thought of independently of classrooms and schools. We fail to realize that children can be taught on the streets, in the home, in playgrounds or in camps, and that the setting is not necessarily the major determinant of the function. Likewise, psychotherapeutic treatment does not have to take place in a particular kind of setting or building, but can be carried out in any place where humans can come together.

And yet we put a great premium on fixed structures and facilities. The plant takes on an almost magical potency for the community. The old complaint of professionals that legislative bodies are willing to buy brick and mortar is probably related to the public's preference for the structural fixing of operational patterns. Such preference makes sense if we accept the "community-defense" hypothesis offered in this book. If the community is moved by a drive to reduce its anxiety level or level of arousal occasioned by disruptive or dissociative human events as much as by a drive to give help, it would be reasonable that patterns tied to clearly visible structures would be preferred to patterns without this structural locus. The very visibility of the structure is reassuring and anxiety reducing, announcing by its observable presence that a concrete defensive structure stands between discordant individuals and the community.

Operational patterns located in physical facilities seem to have agreater chance for continuity of funding and support by the community. Physical plants are not as easily abandoned as programs or operational patterns not located in such structures. The operations of a detached worker, street psychologist, social worker or roving educator would probably not receive the same level of continued public financing or respect that the same operations would if carried on in a fixed facility. Group work done in nonspecific places in human-stress fields of inner cities would probably be at least as effective as that carried out in a settlement house, community center or social-welfare agency; it would, however, not be likely to have continued support from the public and power sectors. Consequently there is a tendency to marry these operations to particular kinds of agency housings.

One of the negatives of this bias toward particular housing forms is that the facilities can too easily become separated from the mainstream of life. They can be easily detached from the rest of the social fields of behavior and become isolated, closed systems with their own esoteric culture that attract little public scrutiny or accountability. Individuals channeled into these closed systems are too easily separated from society and lost to the normal influences of human and social forces. Out of this type of social isolation, such closed systems as state mental hospitals and state prisons can easily become debilitating and arresting influences on the character and life-styles of their human inhabitants.

Characteristics of the Distinguishing Techniques of the Operational Patterns

Behavioral Goals

The operational-delivery patterns of the behavior-regulator systems could also be divided and classified according to the major behavioral goals of their methods and operations. These methods and operations are an intervention into the lives of individuals that grows directly out of the basic assumptions about human behavior entertained by the particular regulator systems. These interventions have more or less specific human effects that they aim to achieve, and these outcomes are direct correlates of the basic assumptions of the regulator system. Therefore the operations or interventions may be described as techniques beginning in basic assumptions about human behavior reinforced in their human effects by the power of the community and terminating when they have achieved some measure of success in the behavioral outcome toward which the assumption is aimed.

The characteristic behavioral goals of the techniques of intervention give the total operational pattern a particular cast that distinguishes it as the operational-delivery apparatus of a particular regulator system. Although an operational pattern does not rely exclusively on a single behavioral goal, its predominant technology has a major identifying goal. These characteristics can be grouped as 1) construction or development, 2) restoration or remediation, 3) containment and punishment, and 4) goal substitution.

Constructive, developmental or catalytic goals of operational patterns

The constructive, developmental or catalytic goals assume certain potentialities in men, certain unrealized capacities, functions and behaviors. In the circumstances toward which the methods are aimed the assumption is that the raw materials of nature are present. Their realization depends primarily on the focused delivery of environmental forces and influences to the organism and on the organism's active integration of these in such a way as to translate potentiality into actuality. In this process, what is now a promise is expected to become a realization. The operational patterns most typical of this emphasis are home, school and church. The process of delivery includes parenting, teaching and ministry. The clearest example is the operational pattern of schools in the educational system of behavior regulation. This typical pattern, built primarily on the method of teaching, devotes itself to the outcome of development, construction or catalysis of human behavior.

Restorative, rehabilitative or remedial goals

There is an almost endless variety of operational patterns built to reconstruct, rehabilitate, reorganize or remediate human behavior of which the community disapproves or that arouses anxiety in the community. Typical behaviors subjected to this approach are mental illness, mental retardation, sexual perversion, crime and cultural deprivation. Patterns in this category include clinics, remedial-education programs and vocational re-habilitation. The medical/mental-health system of behavior regulation, through its operational patterns of hospitals and clinics, is the prototype of this cluster of behavioral goals. The installations of clinics and hospitals are built around the procedures of therapy and healing and aim at restoration of the individual to a former hypothetical state of behavioral health.

Coercive, constraining or punitive goals

Special exile places have in the past been the favored mechanism for removing threatening behaviors and the individual producing them from interactions with the larger community. They have been created for such problems as criminal behavior, mental illness, drug addiction, perversions and alcoholism. This mechanism has also been extensively used in large cities to exclude the contaminating behaviors of aggressive, nonresponsive students. Almost any large urban educational system has special containment schools and classes that dissociate the discordant student from the regular program. The most typical example of patterns with this cluster of coercive, constraining and punitive goals is the legal-correctional system of behavior regulation through prisons, detention centers, training schools and correctional institutions. These patterns are built largely around the methods of controlling authority and policing.

Substitutive, reductive or alternative behavioral goals

Such goals are typical of the techniques of the

multivaried operational-delivery patterns of the social-welfare system. There is a climate of advocacy, succorrance and protection in these patterns. Typical techniques are casework, protective services and economic aid. They attempt to surround behavior with supplements of supports that either cushion its negative aspects or encourage alternative, competing behaviors that can offset the negative ones.

Time Orientation

In their concentration on the behavior of individuals in the community, the operational-delivery patterns of the behavior-regulator systems differ also in their time orientation. In a broad sense, the time orientation of the operational-delivery patterns is derived from the basic assumptions about human behavior that characterize each system. Time orientation can be predominantly past, present or future. The behavior-shaping techniques and operations of the pattern reflect the dominant orientation. Since the technology is the major determinant of the pattern, this orientation permeates the total organizational structure and climate and places its distinctive stamp on the installations representing the specific ecology-regulator system. The dominant time orientation of education, for example, is future behavior. Therefore the operations and total climate of school are predominantly oriented toward the future performance of the organism and future events in its life. The mental-health system is primarily oriented toward past events as the precursors of current behavior and places little importance on current behaviors. Therefore it orients its predominant technology and its clinical or hospital installations to the past of the organism. Its way of dealing with the present reality is constantly to redo the past and to orient the organism continually toward changing its own past history as it affects its present circumstances.

The social-welfare and legal-correctional systems seem to have their major orientation in the present. They do not attempt to redo past history or to delve directly into the future course of events of the organism. Instead their operational patterns have the air of freezing the organism constantly in the present. Prisons, for instance, tend to freeze the past history of the offender in an installation oriented toward current retaliation and current punishment for past events. The organism is treated as a more or less unchanging constellation of events. The apparatus and operations of social welfare's operational-delivery patterns also have been oriented primarily to the current state of the organism. Its operations have not been predominantly designed to change either the past or the future, but seem to be based on an assumption of the present state of the organism's maintaining itself. It is a here-and-now maintenance, a supporting and buttressing orientation.

Target of Entry

Another distinguishing characteristic of the techniques that determine the operational pattern is its target of entry into the problem situation. This target is related to the behavior-regulator system's assumptions about the crucial engagement point for its regulatory efforts and the places where it chooses to concentrate its influence in order to have maximum effect on human behavior. The system's operational-delivery apparatus can direct its operations at the entry point of 1) Interpersonal and intrapersonal events, 2) the setting or context, and 3) behavioral events.

Interpersonal or intrapersonal events

The techniques in this class are directed toward the inner nature of man, toward those factors that are presumed to underlie observable behavior. The psychotherapeutic techniques of mental-health clinics and the teaching techniques of schools can be placed in this class. Operational patterns that employ techniques aimed at this entry target have been quite popular in recent times and have achieved considerable prominence and status in our society. Those factors that were suggested in the first chapter as being responsible for the general revolution in human affairs may also have contributed to the prominence of interpersonal and intrapersonal techniques, such as psychotherapy, group dynamics, counseling, and sensitivity training. The horrors of the historically recent events of man's wholesale destruction of man and the revelations of an inner self that appeared at the same time have given man a new consciousness of his inner depths. Such revelations are causing us to look into ourselves and to examine critically the significance and importance of inner life.

The community setting or circumstances

Another target of entry for the techniques of the operational-delivery patterns is the setting or human stress field out of which disturbing or threatening behavior arises. The purpose of this entry is to change or supplement the context of behavior or to provide a specially designed context that will 1) discourage threatening behavior, or 2) encourage the substitution of community-approved behavior. In a larger sense, the attempt is to modify the environment in such a way as to establish a greater harmony between individual and society. This target of entry has been widely employed by the social-welfare agencies. It is also the major target for newer regulator groups such as economic-opportunity operational patterns and those of housing and urban development. Two of the specific techniques employed at such entry targets are community organization and urban development.

Behavioral events

A number of operational patterns employ behavior itself as their chosen target. They bring their techniques quite directly to bear on the specific behaviors that are creating alarm in the community. This is the typical entry point of the legal-correctional system; with the recent development in psychology of direct behavior-modification technologies, this approach is being more widely used across operational patterns. Behavioral therapy and behavioral training are rapidly rising as important groups of methods for community response to the threatening conduct of individuals.

The Agent of Transaction Between
Person and Society

A Human Being

The ultimate agent of the transaction that occurs at the agency interface between the individual and society is another human being. He is a crucial, living synapse point through which is carried on the bartering and bargaining between persons and communities. The organizational structure of the operational pattern within which he works is intended as the enabling context of his brokerage operations; unfortunately the organizational context frequently takes precedence over the significance of the human agent. Each of the behavior-regulator systems has carefully indoctrinated the transactional agent into its own philosophy, body of knowledge and techniques. The agent performs his assignments in the unique style of the behavior-regulator system that employs him. This style varies from system to system, although the societal-individual mediator role is common to all of them. The style may be that of teacher, policeman, psychotherapist, caseworker or minister.

In the final analysis, the crucial delivery from community into individual and from individual into community must pass through the system of this human transceiver. The civilizing process actually reduces itself to the exchange between two human beings no matter what structures we have created for this purpose. In this respect, the environmental substance and forces presented to the end points of our receptor-effecter mechanisms are not the crucial essence of learning to live in communities. The essence reduces itself to one human touching another human with the intent to influence his development and behavior. The method and value of operational delivery is secondary to reciprocal human engagement. Its value to the unfolding individual potential is like the natural nutrient for the squab that must first be taken into the body of the adult pigeon. The transformation of the external environment occurs not in the operational pattern itself but in the system of the human being who makes the final presentation to the receiving organism.

The training of the human medium for such operational delivery of substance and forces is of considerable importance, but it is not the most crucial factor. Most important is the kind of engagement that the humanizing agent can foster. Some are capable of a quality and depth of engagement that catalyzes and strengthens human potential. Some are capable only of cultural transmission. Some cannot rise above insistence on cultural repression and inhibition. Some are completely incapable of human engagement free of their cultural roles.

Ultimately, however, behavioral and social-science technology is transmitted by a human being. If we put too much emphasis on the particular method or structure by which the individual is being influenced, we are overlooking the significance of the humanizing agent; are disregarding the importance of everything that transpires between the agent mediator and the individual who is being influenced. We are overlooking the tremendous attraction of another human being for the one who is undergoing an experience of change or growth, and we are underestimating the importance of a human model as the central ingredient for human development.

Review

We have tried to sort operational patterns according to their distinguishing characteristics and those of their specialized technology. In spite of these differences, all are part of the behavior-regulation apparatus of the society. All share in the community functions of shaping and regulating human behavior and of trying to harmonize individuals and communities. The operational patterns are not only the operational-delivery arm of the behavior-regulator systems but are also agencies of the community. As such, their methods are infused with the power of the community in influencing the individual. Some patterns, along with the systems within which they operate, are directly linked to the state through its government body, while others, like churches, have no direct government linkages. Some, like schools, have sustained chronology-building responsibility for individual lives, while others, like family service agencies, assume responsibility only under emergency conditions and only for individuals who are producing community emergencies. Some patterns, like community-action programs, are free of clear-cut facility boundaries separating them from the larger community. Others, like mental hospitals or clinics, have distinct physical-structure boundaries and are semiautonomous, behavior-shaping subcommunities within the larger community.

Operational patterns can also be sorted according to the determining characteristics of their techniques. These distinguishing characteristics include behavioral goals, time orientation and target of entry. The techniques' behavioral goals include 1) construction, 2) restoration, and 3) constraint. Their time orientations include the past events in the life of the organism, the future of the organism and the present state of the organism. The targets of entry include 1) intrapersonal and interpersonal factors, 2) the setting or field surrounding behavior, and 3) observable behavioral events themselves.

It was pointed out that the crucial agent of delivery in the operational pattern is another human being. It is his representation of himself and the community that harmonizes the forces of the individual and the forces of the community at the interface of the operational pattern. The tendency to place our operational-delivery emphasis on the behavior-regulation structure and the behavior-regulating techniques has interfered with the significant process of human exchange as the *modus operandi* of civilization. Such a process of minimizing the nutrient and social-representative function of the human agent is alienating the individual from the society.

Definitions

The definition of systems, given earlier in this exploration, extends to the operational patterns and the subpro-
grams of these patterns. At this point it is worth while
to state again the definition as it specifically applies to
the patterns. A behavior-shaping operational pattern is
an action configuration of 1) a set of basic assumptions
about human behavior, 2) a body of behavioral or
human-science knowledge, 3) a set of methods or techniques that apply the assumptions and knowledge to human
behavior, and 4) a group of professional agents trained in
the first three components who intercede in human lives in
behalf of the community.

II

A New Climate of Radical Change

Review of the Threat-Recoil Thesis

The book's general thesis presented up to this point is that any human agency is part of a much larger infrastructure within society. This infrastructure is profoundly influenced by an interlocked field of forces that constantly plays on it and shapes its actions and directions. This field of focus is made up of threat excitation, a medium of cultural doctrine, threat response and power. The interlock between threat exciters and threat responders, joined with the power structures through the medium of cultural doctrine, provides the energy force that creates and maintains a pathology or trouble orientation within the behavior-regulator structures. It deflects the constructive and creative interactions between the infrastructure and

99

human targets into relatively unproductive channels. This deflection takes the form of repressing the threat-exciter sectors and/or soothing the anxiety of the threat-responder sectors without bringing about a resolution within and between them and the society.

A New Factor

Now, however, a new factor has appeared in this arena: a profound state of human foment about the nature of human existence and human communities. The foment is beginning to act on the gestalt of the existing field of trouble forces and the existing regulator infrastructure to introduce a climate of change and revision within them. Some of the most impregnable cultural doctrines and taboos are being breached; sanctified dogma about human behavior is being questioned. The institutional edifices founded on such doctrine and dogma are beginning to undergo sweeping changes in their actions and structures. The whole infrastructure of behavior regulation is involved in this eruption of change. It is beginning to loosen and give and to try to incorporate new human forms and new human thought. It is becoming more concerned about human rights and human needs and is trying to remove some of its own blinders to see the field of human trouble with new eyes, new views. Some of the changes in cultural legend and behavioral dogma are beginning to invade the formerly rigid stabilization of the field of trouble forces that held the infrastructure in its orbit. The interactions between the threat elicitors and the threat responders are being changed because the definition of the nature of threat is being changed. Changes in sexual lore, religious lore and the lore of love and hate, play and irrationality are all under reexamination. Therefore the cultural doctrines, proscriptions and behavioral taboos are being revised.

With the revision of beliefs about human nature, human rights and human behavior, the agencies that transacted the exchanges between threat elicitors and threat responders are being changed. Structures such as social welfare, legal correction and education are all caught up in this sweep. Much more definitive changes are probably in store. Our society and our psyche will have to be adjusted to these new concepts and rates of change. We will have to build adaptive mechanisms into the regulators themselves in order to master this massive revolution in human life. It is not possible to describe all of the rapid changes and revisions that are occuring and are likely to occur. The remaining chapters will sketch some of these in process. It will point out some of the structural changes that are already beginning to occur and suggest others that are needed or that are likely to occur.

6

Conditions for Changes
in the Regulator Network

Signs of Dissatisfaction

Against the vast psychosocial upheavals that are sweeping across the world, special rumblings and tremors are occuring at the site of the regulator apparatus. These protests suggest that the civilizing process conducted through this apparatus has not sufficiently modulated incompatibilities between man and man, and between man and his behavioral environment. Deficiencies in the regulator process and functions are beginning to show up in many ways. They are indicated, for instance, by such evidence as the increasing psychosocial tension arising from the ineffectiveness of our society and its dominant culture in accommodating numerous denigrated idiocultures such as the Negroes, Puerto Ricans, Appalachians,

103

Indians, Mexican-Americans and Cajuns. Individuals within these idiocultures, by virtue of their identification with and integration into their own referent groups, find themselves socially incompetent and alienated. This incompetence holds true when they are treated and measured by the standards and requirements of the larger society. They also occupy grounds or territories that are being increasingly identified as hazardous environments in modern communities. These weddings between hazardous environments and vulnerable population groups are in turn creating numerous social-stress fields, such as inner-city blight and rural slums.

In the past history of communities, education and other human-supportive services have been major agents for counteracting and moderating such effects. Education was the great equalizer and welder. Now there is some question as to whether these organizations are as effective as they once were. There may even be the question of whether they are having negative effects on the idiocultures and their environing conditions. Some of these cultural groups are making this claim, typically in their wholesale condemnation of police and the corrective apparatus.

There seems to be a vast centrifugal tendency operating in society that shatters communities into multiple discordant social cells and dissociated individuals. The regulator apparatus seems relatively ineffective in counteracting this tendency. It is as though devisive and destructive forces have taken precedence over constructive and agglutinating forces in communities. Something seems to have gone awry with the active binding power of regulator agencies. They seem unable to exert sufficient centripetal influence on communities to counteract the more or less natural separating process in community living. Another sign of deficiencies in the regulator functions is the rising stridency of threat-recoil storms associated with individual behaviors or discordant groups. The spiraling costs in money and manpower over one divergent category after the other, such as the suicidal, homicidal, sexual deviant or delinquent, suggest that revisions are required. These revisions probably include both our thinking and our actions with respect to life in human environments.

Within the framework of this analysis of the situation, the critical role of the regulator infrastructure takes on new significance. The apparatus must be rejuvenated so that it can more effectively produce constructive coadaptation between individuals and their environment. There are many indications that society is awakening to both the importance and the deficiencies in this infrastructure. The awakening can be seen, for instance, in the protests and attacks of poorly served recipients on school and welfare-department programs. Another indicator is minor revolts within the regulator agencies against calcified human ideologies and practices. The dissent of nuns and priests in the Catholic Church is an example of such minor revolts. Still another indicator of increasing consciousness of the role of the regulator infrastructure is the recent / flood of new legislation that either creates new regulatory agencies or invites radical modification of old ones.

Relationship to the Larger Picture of Social Unrest

The crisis in relevancy and adequacy of the regulator infrastructure was probably precipitated and is certainly being intensified by the movement of man into a new psychosocial reality. This reality no longer has the appearance of a simple relationship between a physical being and a physical world. It is moving very fast into a relationship of the psychological self to a world that has developed psychological depths and dimensions. Old patterns of behavior regulation have become limited and relatively ineffective in helping man toward this new relationship to the world characterized by a shifting of balance in the juxtaposing of human and societal rights. The basic psychological demands of human beings, in their greater depths, have emerged as an insistent part of the whole, which refuses to be denied and cannot be denied if man is to survive. Prior to this era, psychological rights and depths could be ignored and displaced. The multiple facets of our psychological selves that were at variance with society could be concealed from ourselves and from the relevant others. They could be transmuted into external environmental problems and physical dimensions and struggled with on the physical and environmental plane. Although never really separated from us and our daily lives, our psychological reality could be buried or hidden from view. We could project socially troubling urges away from their inner source in our psychological makeup and into the behavior of undesirable populations.

Now this projection is no longer possible. We have begun to recognize ourselves in the rejected other. We have caught glimpses of our internal quarrel with society in the social defiance and social incompetency of others. We are now beginning to ask questions regarding the extent to which society can and should restrain the expression of our psychological selves. Undue restraints on the self have become oppressive and binding. We are moving even beyond the relatively enlightened, yet limited concepts saying that the man who could not bring the forces of his inner self into an adjustment with the existing world was either criminal or sick. We are moving beyond insistence on repression, suppression and subjugation of vast inner life areas as a sufficient and necessary condition for survival in the social world. We now ask that social reality be modulated to accommodate and recognize the fuller scope of our inner being and inner requirements rather than continue a disproportionate insistence on accommodation of inner being to a disembodied external social reality. We are aware that the bomb and the extermination camps are not chance external mutants, but that they have issued directly from our inner nature. We are aware that the antidote must come from the wellsprings of constructive and affectional urges within us, rather than exclusively from modification of purely external conditions of the environment.

It is as though a part of our inner nature, long submerged, is being recognized as important, determining our environing context. This new state of existence makes long-controlled personal worlds a part of public life; it makes the inner world of others an important and significant fact of life. In this new state, there is an accompanying feeling of strangeness and an accompanying mobilization of psychological and community defenses against the emergence. The strangeness is awesome and bewildering to us. In such a condition of anomie, there is a greater need than ever for the artificial behavior regulators to come to man's aid and support him through the difficult insights that are growing and gaining significance and to guard him against the agony of decompensation that comes with this flood of insight. If he is to tolerate himself, man must have help with the self, outside supports to see him through this transition period. The behavior-regulator systems must find ways to come to terms with the recognition and public release of the previously subterranean qualities of self into the exposed and relatively unprepared community. We must find ways for revelations about our inner nature to be absorbed and creatively employed in reconstruction of the external environment with mass chaos or mass ego-defense collapse.

Testing Ground for Change

A major testing ground for renovation of the regulators to fit the changing relationship between self and community should be at the sites of the rejected and unintegrated segments of society. Regulatory systems that can modify the community environment and its climate to accommodate constructively the life-styles and insistent personal claims of these groups are much more likely to be aligned to the new relationship between man and his world. Systems that can modulate these groups and the dislocations of their lives into effective associations with society are much more likely to embrace the full scope of the unengaged and unsatisfied portions of self, the social significance of which has gone unrecognized and underground so long.

If our psychological nature is to be given new access and acceptability in the structures of society, we must begin with the denigrated populations. In finding a way for them to live a community life, we will discover a way for ourselves. Our existing defensive crisis reaction to solutions employed by our regulator apparatus no longer appears to work. There are too many who are joining the ranks of socially excluded and alienated populations and therefore too many threat exciters to ward off or control. The discovery of their counterparts in ourselves is making it more and more difficult to draw lines between them and us. They now become people like ourselves who represent the early signals of what the whole population may be becoming. The situation is ripe. We must prove, on their grounds, that we are capable of bringing society and individuals into a supportive and mutually beneficial relationship around these unsolved psychological problems. Our deepening awareness of the dissociation between our own social facade and our inner nature makes our former process of displacement on or scapegoating of the threat-exciter groups less and less successful. In discovering mutual similarities, we are recognizing that the agony of their lives is a slightly distorted mirror reflection of the plight of the larger mass of relatively integrated culture bearers. It is here that we must solve our problem or face the prospect of a continued spread of dissociation and ever-widening circles of rejected and excluded groups.

We cannot go on indefinitely creating new negative categories for threat provokers and new protective programs to reduce their impact on us. Nor can we blindly insist solely on the adaptation of the individual to the artificial environment of the communities we have built for him to live in. Along with our insistence on compliance with the world as it is, we must also gradually moderate the artificial environment in ways that complement the self of man. At the same time that we press the claims of society on him, we must constantly invent and construct environmental supports for his deeper psychological claims on society. We must develop the instruments of reciprocity between the threat-provoking culture violators and the threat-responsive culture bearers. If it is necessary to insist on accommodation of the threat provokers to the culture, then it is also necessary to moderate the culture bearers in ways that make them less sensitive to threat and more accepting of wide bands of human nuances within themselves and others. A gradual transformation of this sort requires inventive redesign of the regulatory apparatus that facilitates the coadaptation between the individual and his community. Much more precise knowledge about the management of human behavior will have to be generated by the behavioral, social and mental-health scientists before we can proceed with this task with any feeling of certainty. The regulator apparatus will have to be rejuvenated as our own invented instrument of reciprocity between individual and societal claims.

Fluid Deployment of Regulator Forces

Changes in the Regulator Apparatus

Conditions may already be gathering for a major reconstruction of the form and direction of the regulator apparatus and the process of behavior management. Social necessity and social crisis seem to be pressing for reformation in the feudalism of regulator agencies and proprietary claims on segmented aspects of human lives. It is beginning to be evident, for instance, that the nature of life problems is not split into separated, unrelated territories within the human organism or the human environment in the same way that agencies have divided these aspects. Therefore the existing practice of strongly specialized, differentiated, prerogative-determined agencies and operational patterns is becoming a relatively unnatural and economically burdensome organization of human supportive resources. Until recently, the locus of program determination, the fulcrum of determination of manpower use, and the mandates for installation building seemed to flow directly from inside the separate specialized proprietary services rather than from the nature of the human-problem situations themselves. The internal requirements of agencies have played a major role in shaping social-service policy and operations.

The current social upheavals may change this situation. The major force for determining the nature and form of human-service programs is beginning to be relocated in the center of human-problem situations in their natural setting and to grow out of the problem situation itself. This recentering of operational requirements away from the internal organization and out to the external problem could result in some rather drastic changes in the present territorial prerogatives of agencies. First, it could reconstitute the structures and boundaries of the separate agencies in ways that would more truly reflect the merged and interlocking nature of human troubles in their own settings. New types of mergers of agency forces and agency programs could be formed to bring multifaceted resources to bear on the compounded human-societal problems in the living community. Second, the forces and structure of the reconstituted regulator agencies could assume a more fluid and mobile form, just as the problems in situs have a fluid and changing form. Central-office-designed and technologically forced program operations have been too inflexible and too immobile to come to grips with the problem situation in the community field of forces acting directly on the troubled individuals. In their place, probably will come programs that flow directly from and move in fluid fashion alongside the human problems and human situations as they stream through their complex environments and contexts. Hard and fast lines among procedures, services and personnel may have to give way to elastic and shifting boundaries flowing to meet the ever-changing shapes of the problems.

Third, the present consolidation of program authority into unitary and individual sources will probably be modified to provide both for group authority and shifting authority patterns. Rather than residing in single individuals, agency authority would reside in groups and group balances and would probably shift according to the change in needs in the field; field authority would rise to greater prominence in decision making and policy determining. Fourth, the highly centralized nature of regulator agencies and operational patterns may give way to decentralized patterns and smaller units distributed more broadly than they now are. Along with this, much of the centralized staff residing in the agencies' internal feudal compounds would probably have to be moved outside their walls and be deployed in the field on which the problems of human and societal forces are engaged. In this way, personnel would be more directly in contact with the shape and nature of the multilevel and varied human problems they face. In this way also, the internal operations and programs that issue from the authority sources would be more likely to be an accurate reflection of the situation in the field.

Such major changes in operational patterns would be very difficult to bring about under ordinary circumstances. The current psychosocial and cultural unrest, however, may be pressing for such reconstruction. In this state of unrest, there appears to be a rather important change occurring in the linkages between the public, power and agency triad in the larger society that will make drastic modifications in the agency pattern quite possible.

A Balance-Wheel Apparatus

Until recently, the impacted power interlock that bound together the culture-bearing public, operational patterns and political structures served restricted social ends. This interlock appeared to be utilized, in large measure, to alleviate fear and segregate or restrain cultural deviation. Now, in the new field of forces, a dynamic flux is occurring in the interlock, and there is some loosening up of the impacted power within it. The dissolving of the power impact seems to be apparent in the political structures' recent efforts to make massive use of new scientific knowledge about human conditions. They seem to be pressing for problem resolution rather than problem suppression and are demanding an accounting from the regulator agencies with regard to their problem-resolution success or lack of success.

In this flux we are seeing some of the alienated groups both being allocated and securing a greater proportionate share of social power. Human rights are not only being recognized, but many movements are afoot to ensure their legitimation. Thus these alienated groups are no longer treated as mere wards of society but as participants in the increase of their own social salience. They are perceived as more than recipients of social largess, as important elements of the population in their own right. For its part, the culture-bearing public is lifting some of the cultural restraints that it has imposed on itself. It is recognizing the human similarities between the concealed portion of itself and the life-styles of the alienated groups. It is facing rather than denying the nature of the psychosocial problems that have both been created by and resulted in great social bastions of self-denial and self-condemnation. Thus there is growing up a renewed empathy for the most obviously maladapted among us.

In this flux also, the operational patterns of the behavior-regulator systems are being shifted in their position vis-à-vis the political structures, the culture-bearing public and the socially extruded exciters. The operational patterns may now move into a new position of balance wheel in the psychobehavioral relationships among these various sectors. Out of the authority of its rapidly expanding knowledge, the behavior-regulator apparatus may begin to moderate the psychosocial relationships and reciprocities among the political, public and threatening sectors. It may monitor and even help to adjust these relationships when they deflect too far in any single sector direction.

Relationship to Power

The apparatus may relate itself in a new way to the

political structures by more deliberately becoming an educator to this structure concerning the substance of the evolving knowledge of human beings and human needs. It may help the power structure by constantly feeding into it substantive human and social information that could become the basis for the development of social policy at the administrative, judicial and legislative levels. It may become more and more an instrument of human-knowledge nourishment to this structure and less and less a political instrument for control of fear and restraint of alienated groups. In some cases, the systems may have to learn to take scientific positions that are not directly aligned with the political positions and political exigencies of the power structure at the moment. They may more deliberately bring their substantive authority into public dialogue with the political authority of the governing structures when these structures wittingly or unwittingly violate human needs and human psychological rights.

The agencies' persisting organizational pattern seems to be structured for maximum continuity between the political-power sector and the professionals within the agencies and operational patterns of the regulator systems. The agency head is directly responsible to the political administration in office, and the delegated-authority lines beneath him flow downward in a perpendicular line pattern. In this fusion, the front line of the agency, in closest proximity to the exciter, has to be most immediately responsible to the executive pyramid and executive needs of the organization rather than to its designated constituency. This is an efficient form of organization for a primarily unilateral alliance between the political sector and the regulator systems to form a protector barrier for the culture-bearing public against the threat exciters. If agencies, however, are to exercise multilateral problem-solving responsibility for the bal-ancing of the three — public, political and exciter — a different organizational form would seem to be required.

The highly structured pyramidal authority lines that give dominance to administrative and power concerns within the major agencies would have to be remodeled to allow for more horizontal authority and for frequent, flexible redistribution of authority according to the need to shift priorities, missions and target groups. This should allow for substantive considerations' having equal influence on the program activities of the institution. It should also allow for concentration of time, brains and energy toward the deepening, expansion and development of the substance on which the agency is based, rather than on the immediate contingencies of the administrative and political-power field. Substance would then become the major power determinant. When substance blossomed in a particular area, power would be attracted to and radiate from that substantive area, rather than solely from administrative slots. Thus power could shift and be redistributed as substance shifts and develops.

If the agency is to be responsive to the psychological realities of individuals, those workers who are in direct contact with the exciter sector must have some influence in the psychosocial policy decisions of the agency. Their emotional and attitudinal understanding, their immersion in the lives of the exciter-client group, their interpretation of the situation are more thoroughly conversant with the living phenomenon toward which they are oriented. This type of feed-in and representation would keep the agency attuned to the actual human situation and responsive to the gestalt of ecological problems that it is supposed to regulate. Agencies very badly need this anchor and advocacy base in the rejected populations to keep alive their substantive knowledge about human behavior. This emphasis also would assure a continuing dialectic between the power and love mixture that constitutes the human roots of regulator organizations.

The humanistic orientation of the agency representative who directly encounters the suffering of people is the lifeblood of behavior-regulator systems. In the present vertical structures, these representatives are too frequently weaned away from their basic emphathic orientation by the realities of the unequal distribution of organizational rewards in favor of administrative power positions. In the frustration of their thwarted contributions at the decision-making table, they too frequently abandon their emphatic orientation in exchange for power slots in the vertical structure of the agency. New ways should be found to keep their roots deepening and growing in the living community and to assure that their efforts, ideas and solutions will have a measure of salience in the operations of the agency.

One way that might modify the unilateral power preoccupation of the agencies' top hierarchy would be to develop a change in concept of the executive staff. In addition to occupying the seats of authority in the agency, executives could spend a reasonable portion of their time giving direct service. During the period of this part-time role, the executive would step down from his office and return to such roles as caretaker, problem solver and healer. This would keep him in touch with the raw material of problem conditions and the stress field. It would keep the elements of human suffering and environmental strain fresh in his mind and in his thinking about agency functioning. It would give him a chance to be free of full-time administrative and power operations and allow him a chance to continue to develop the other facets of his skills that might otherwise deteriorate without exercise. This might also give the executive the kind of perspective that would subsume both the point of view and attitudes of those in the power structure and the point of view of those who are seen as discordant or alien.

Within this bilateral perspective, it may be possible for him to interpret more clearly the nature of problems. It would also guard against the natural tendency of taking on the coloration of the group with which he associates most frequently. He could maintain an independence of thought and a total view that includes the direct knowledge of experience in both levels.

The loosening of the tight, vertical authoritative structure by agencies and other operational patterns would also tend to increase their flexibility and their ability to move with the stream of events in the life space of communities. They would be in a better position to shift their focus, quickly realign their various substantive resources and forces, and easily mobilize their energies in light of shifting exigencies in the general social situation, in target populations and in purposes. They would be more able to assume the role of psychosocial balance wheel among the political-power, culture-bearing and exciter sectors.

Guild Limits

In order to attain such flexibility, the agencies and other operational patterns would also have to loosen some of their strong power ties to single professional guilds and begin to cross freely guild lines in seeking substance and consultation. Multiple guild associations would be required in order to capitalize on and gain maximum utilization of varying philosophies about human behavior, variegated bodies of knowledge, wider reservoirs of leadership talent, and the greater scope of technological capacities for operational delivery. In general, such alliances would also provide the agencies with multiple sources of professional power and many different alternatives for their functioning. It is probable that the encapsulated professional-guild system has reached its peak and is on the decline and that it may be supplanted by some sort of consortium form of professionalism. The days in which the operating agencies both supported the strength of the guilds and were more or less captives of single guilds may be on their way out. The old-line single-guild agencies and operational patterns are being supplemented rapidly with operational patterns that cut across guild lines, such as some of the poverty, housing and urban-affairs programs.

We will probably soon see many other types of amalgamated operational patterns in which a number of professions or agencies come together under a common umbrella to tackle the multiple nature of human behavioral problems. These kinds of organizations and programs will not support the type of guild control we have known up until now. Even more important, the tenor of the times cannot tolerate the partitioning off of human problems into guild jurisdictions and guild territories. It cannot support the ownership by a single guild of a body of knowledge, a program of training and indoctrination, and a set of technologies.

New Ventures in Managing Stress and Strain

In the present climate of human resurgence and social fluidity, older approaches to relief of stress and strain in the exchange between individuals and their environs are being joined by fresh and flexible kinds of responses to human-problem conditions. Alongside the giant establishments of the old agencies, we are seeing the sudden emergence of new and unofficial agency forms. They are spontaneous, fluid and ever-changing forms, which mold themselves to the stream of psychosocial events and strains in the changing community. These new organizations do not put total reliance on hard-structured and formal solutions. Instead, these unofficial, semiofficial and even self-appointed agencies mold themselves to the dynamic flux of human stress fields. Their engagement is through organizational structures that have the free-flowing form of an amoeba.

Many communities are becoming impatient with the limitations of old regulator agencies and are beginning to shift some of their tactics. Instead of placing their total reliance on the older, monolithic agencies, they are starting to diversify some of their resources and consigning a portion of these to multiple chains of minor and major social experiments. Even within the established professionals there is a faint beginning of new directions. Instead of concentrated hardening of professional methods and technology, there is a tendency to encourage spontaneous approaches to the problem stream of human events. This is a cautious trend, not universally acceptable among professionals; here and there across the country, however, there are signs of increasing flexibility. Instead of total insistence on ideological purity, divergences from professional dogma are beginning to be countenanced. Instead of uniform preoccupation with role specification and insistence on legal definition and fixing of role, some role diversification and role experimentation are being allowed. It is possible that in this current era of psychosocial transformation in the human condition, we may be about to enter into a new period of discovery and recovery in the process of behavioral management. Conditions seem to be favorable for a decided change in the total infrastructure of behavior regulation.

7

Entering the Relationship
Between Exciter and Responder

In human-behavior problem areas in the past, agencies have directed their efforts largely toward the exciter as a host carrier of pathological propensities or actions. This is only a partial analysis of the problem to which agencies must address themselves. Now, instead of isolating the exciter as the exclusive host of the pathology, regulator programs are beginning to try to redirect some of their efforts and attention to the threat-exciter, threat-responder dyad and to the stressed territorial field that accentuates their discord. The past tendency to concentrate exclusively on the exciter and the field of stressful forces surrounding him failed to take into account the contributions of the responder and the mutual nature of the engagement between exciters and responders. In addressing themselves to the mutually induced disturbance of the threat-exciter, threat-responder dyad, the regulator agencies may achieve new perspectives on old problems. They may, for instance, view slums as human-stress-field territories whose forces participate directly in the antipathetic exciter-responder relationship. Other environmental contexts could be viewed in the same way. A disturbed home, classroom, office or organization could be viewed as more circumscribed stress fields that surround and participate in a mutual clash of human associations.

The agencies may abandon some of their buffer and protective efforts and attempt to focus their solutions on the stress field and the engagement of the participants that constitute the problem. It must look two ways at once. At the same time that it functions in behalf of the political body and public body to seek accommodation of the exciter to the society and to the integrating aspects of his culture, it may also help free the culture bearer from tyrannizing and demeaning aspects of his own culture, particularly from those harsh aspects that cause him to be overbearing and repressive toward his inner nature and toward those who depart from cultural repressions. In looking two ways at once, the regulator agency may offer special external aids to the alienated threat-exciter groups. Where there is social inadequacy the agency may help develop social competence; where there are defects in the environment that stunt and prevent growth or retard the development of threat exciters, corrective efforts may be instituted. A more salutary milieu may be provided such groups and individuals.

The same order and organization that exists in the territorial surroundings of the culture bearer may gradually be extended to the alienated groups. Environmental supports and environmental prostheses may be devised to keep the threatening groups functioning as a part of an open society no matter what their limitations appear to be. Deliberately segregated living situations in all their forms, whether ghettos or incarcerating institutions, may gradually be dissolved. The past psychosocial defense of exiling large numbers of threat-exciter individuals to extrusion colonies such as asylums, prisons, detention centers, jails, mental hospitals and training schools has fostered a costly and proliferating burden on society. This burden has the potential for overwhelming our economic and caretaking manpower capabilities. The population explosion, combined with the current trend toward multiplying the social-extrusion categories, makes the exiling defense a costly and unmanageable solution to psychosocial threat. Socially segregated territorial enclaves like ghettos and socioeconomically exclusive neighborhoods are also becoming hopelessly outmoded psychological solutions as the population grows, as land becomes scarce, and as the demand for recognition of human rights becomes more insistent. Therefore the protective borders between territories should be gradually opened to a free flow of exchanges of all life forms.

An open community may be central to integrated lives. This requires a free environment, where humans of all stripes and persuasions coexist in the same area, where few artificial psychosocial distinctions place fences to shut out those who differ in quality or kind. Static enclaves harboring clusters of homogenous economic, social, psychological, ethnic, religious and social sects have a tendency to result in divisiveness. They create friction borders and no-man's lands between groups and segregate individuals along a dimension of relatively desirable and undesirable kinds. They divide the community into slums and nonslums, into turfs and attitudinal animosities that are almost equivalent to the artificial partitioning of an occupied territory by multilateral occupational forces. People are more likely to be brought into psychological community when they live in each other's presence and when direct confrontation and an attitudinal working through is possible. We should have living representatives of our internal variability and contradictions holding before us the mirror of ourselves so that there will be less fantasied horror and more direct free choice for the possible living out of the contradictory urges within us. If the actual possibility of living out these variegated internal propensities were available in the real environment and in tolerated life examples, such rich psychological profusion would make a person's life-style choice more his own rather than an imposed condition in which he is locked as a prisoner of his psychological caste. A truly open community would randomly distribute the representatives of each of the varied ways of life across the inhabited area.

Although a necessary condition, cohabitation in and of itself is not enough. Common living is only the precondition for mutual cultivation. The clashes that constitute mutual violation should be gradually transformed into a productive engagement between the two sectors. In order to accomplish this, it would be necessary for the culture bearer to be provided with insight into his internal defenses against his behavioral propensities. He would have to become aware of the reasons that cause the behavior of others to be threatening to him.

At the same time that the regulator apparatus orients itself toward the interactions between the environment and the threat exciter, it could also turn a portion of its resources to the threat-responder sector of society. If the threat exciter can be seen as a victim of a depriving and dehumanizing environment, the culture bearer can also be seen as a victim of the "despotism of custom." At the same time that an attempt is being made to bring about a rapprochement between the rejected populations and the environment, a recognition should be made of the role of the culture bearer in the general disturbance. Some of the present efforts expended by agencies in protecting the culture bearer from the encroachment of the threat exciter should be redistributed to provide the culture bearer with an understanding of his relationship to the exciter. There could be a reduction in the effort expended by the agencies in helping the culture bearer deny himself to and defend himself against his internal nature. To this end, the environmentally sustained fictions, outlived truths and historical legends about human behavior and human motivations should be continuously reexamined. Wherever private behavioral practices are contrary to public cultural codes, these human facts should be brought out into the open. In the case of human motivations, for instance, the major legends about man's libidinal and destructive forces or propensities should be publicly revised as new knowledge moderates them.

The school, the church, the home and the clinic should continually reopen conventional beliefs about human living and behavior and should continually modify their teachings and influences according to such changing knowledge. The culture bearer should be systematically extricated from excessive and debilitating fear of individual differences. He should be taught to tolerate wide ranges of variation in behaviors and life-styles and divergent tendencies within himself. At the same time that cognitive approaches are being used to help him increase his tolerance of differences in others, psychological renewal approaches should be employed to help him free himself from the excessive internalized cultural restraints and cultural conditionings that oppress him.

Revising the Cultural Repository

A method could be developed for continuous revision of the historical repository of the culture. Constant reexamination of major beliefs and sanctions could become an institutionalized process. This could be accomplished by taking the expanding body of knowledge about human behavior and human motivation out of the realm of the professional community and into the public marketplace and public communication media. The public could be educated, along with the professional community, with respect to new horizons of thought about human psychology.

The psychosocial sciences differ from the physical sciences in that their scientific knowledge must be translated into living by all individuals involved in the human enterprise. The physical sciences can be held in public trust by a few scientists. Thus the body of knowledge and the explorations of the nature of the human being could be used by society as a basis for examining traditional beliefs transmitted through the culture. Scientific knowledge, like that of the Kinsey and Masters and Johnson studies of sexual behavior, could be shared and judged jointly by the scientist and the public. It could be communicated and interpreted with all of the cautions of scientific method by the human scientists to the mass public. It would thus become a joint enterprise between the public and the human science of continued self-recovery, self-discovery and education.

It would become very important to develop a number of forums for this continuing education of the public about its psychosocial nature. Tabooed behaviors, for example, could be publicly examined and developed into public scientific dialogues on the front page of newspapers. News stories of threat-provoking behaviors could be accompanied by detailed disclosures of scientific theory and research concerning such behavior. The sexual scandals that so frequently rock political parties could provide occasions for public dialogue and public lectures about the nature of such behavior and its prototypes in all of us. Murder, teen rumbles, racial conflicts, and embezzlement could not only be reported through the communication media, but could be accompanied by social, behavioral and mental-health science information about such forms of human behavior.

Sharing of the current psychosocial knowledge with the public could become part of scientific responsibility. The public would have to be trusted to grasp the tentative and unfolding quality of such knowledge just as the college freshman is so trusted. Library shelves, professional journals and cloistered laboratories could become ancilliary repositories of knowledge about human living, and the public marketplace could become its major repository. If wide-scale public communication about the evolving conceptions of human living became easily available to the total society, it is quite possible that the logic-tight thinking and compartmentalized beliefs and prejudices that now characterize our civilization would undergo some change. At least the total society would be widely exposed to the constant influence of quality education about human nature and human existence. As a result, citizens could become much more sanguine and much more sophisticated in the depth and range of human qualities.

Transcending Territorial Boundaries

The territorial boundaries between the public majority and its denigrated groups could be made much more permeable than they are now. Boundaries could be blurred and a constant dialogue of exchange between the dominant culture bearers and alienated groups could be instituted and maintained by the behavior-regulator systems. It could become part of the society's ethos to encourage a continual crossing over of the categorical boundaries. Some of the new measures currently being employed for this purpose could be proliferated. The engagement of middle-class youth in human-service functions in slum neighborhoods, the use of mature middle-class women as tutors to culturally disadvantaged children or as preceptors to culturally disadvantaged mothers, the long-term adoption of disruption-prone slum families by resilient and therapy-sensitized middle-class families, and the use of young adult middle-class males as big brothers to disadvantaged teen-agers are means of encouraging such an exchange. All of these and many other exchange relationships could become institutionalized in our society.

Conversely, we could invent ways for the alienated groups to reciprocate in the life-teaching process. American society has been strengthened in the past through the melting-pot permeability that has blended many cultural strains into society. This capacity, which seems to have been lost or to have diminished in this country, could somehow be reestablished. A minor example of the remaining capacity is the blending of the Negro musical idiom and the hillbilly country-music idiom into the art form of modern American music. Another minor example, limited to the exchange between professional and threat-exciter groups, is found in the therapy exchange between professional and client. The schizophrenic and the paranoid have taught the sensitive, clinically trained professional much about himself and his blindness to societal imperfections and tyrannies. In this way the "patient" has helped the "doctor" recover parts of himself and parts of his buried social insights that would never have been unearthed without the reciprocal tutelage.

Power for the Divergent

Alien groups of all kinds could continue to develop their own power base so that they could attain positions in which they would play a more equal part in determining what is done to and for them by the behavior-regulator systems and their caretaking agencies. The psychologically sick, the criminal, the socially deviant have little to say about the various programs and institutions that are established to help them. All of the threat-exciter, alienated individuals and groups are at the mercy of the determinations made by the political structures, the agency structures and the threatened public majority with respect to the services that they need. They are cast in the rather helpless position of social-disease-carrying wards of the state.

Just as single-industry and cross-industry trade unions have been formed to represent and protect the economic interests of the laborer, single-category and cross-category unions of threat exciters could serve the self-interest of these alienated individuals with respect to their own psychosocial claims on the society. They could be active participants in their fate rather than powerless recipients of the prescriptions meted out to them by the trisector alliance of politician, public and regulator system. With their own psychosocial claims unions the divergents and aliens could provide a new gravitational pull that could free the regulator apparatus from a narrowly constrained orbit in the political and public domains and allow it to move into a true pivotal position in the society at large. Such unions could also separate the substance of the eco-logical sciences from political considerations and allow agency personnel whose primary allegiance is to their con-stituent group to have a greater share in determining the types of program operations that will be carried out by the agency.

If such psychosocial claims unions could be established, it would be much more possible for the regulator apparatus to utilize fully objective indexes of discordant behavior. Too frequently, our current categories of discordance are overdetermined by public and political opinion. Under present circumstances, the threatened sectors, in spite of their benign intentions, are in a privileged position for deciding who is discordant and who is not. With the redistribution of influence, the psychosocial sciences would have greater freedom in arriving on an impartial criterion for determination of pathological forces in the society and in individuals. As an example of such a self-interest group, the ex-hospital-patient clubs could be redirected toward assuming change-agent responsibility for revitalization of state hospitals and related mental-health structures. This self-interest group could develop into a power bloc to press for reform and change in state hospitals and for shared responsibility in determining the content and structure of services to the mentally ill. This is a very knowledgeable group, having a high level of self-investment in the pursuit of mental health and a mentally healthy environment. They could perform a vital service for the rest of us who are so distracted by other pressing problems and demanding roles.

III

The Challenge to our Existence: Postscript

The End of an Era

A strong voice of discontent has arisen inside the human psyche. It takes many forms and has many names. It can be seen in specific thrusts of social action in response to specific kinds of human behavior. It can be seen in the specialized government and world organizations that are instruments of the voice. It shows itself in strong social movements that are enlisting a major share of human energies and the world's social forces. It is a voice that expresses, at the same time that it provokes, the turbulence of our inner selves and outer community casings.

Something new in man's history seems to be occurring.

He has created a technical reality that has ended one era. It could be the end of an eon. Man can now commit suicide en masse. He can now accomplish on a worldwide scale what he has always been able to do as an individual. At the same time, there appears to be the inception of a new force, a great surge from within man, pressing his inner content outward. What was private knowledge is now becoming public; what was hidden and obscure is becoming open and revealed. The surging contractions may be only the heavings of nausea or terror at the sight of what man has created. On the other hand, they may be birth pangs, the urgent flood of life into the world to reassert its claims on the nature of man. Life may be rushing again to struggle with death in that eternal life-death conflict posed so dramatically by Freud. But whatever the source, we seem to be launched into a new era, an era in which our intrapsychic life is being admitted very rapidly into our extrapsychic milieu. The compartmental barriers we had erected against comprehensive knowledge of ourselves have become weakened and permeable, and tremendous shifts and changes are taking place within us.

Among other influences, the events at Auschwitz and Hiroshima shocked us into recognition of the cleavage between behavioral legends and human facts. We were faced with the crippling culture we had fashioned to hide this cleavage. Those awesome events precipitated stunning revelations, and their impact opened us to ourselves in ways that had not previously been possible. Torn loose from our self-deceiving image of ourselves, we were swept up into the consequent storm of our inner world. The brilliance of the nuclear holocaust provided harsh, momentary glimpses of all manner of our human urges and behaviors, which we had suspended in a limbo of pretended nonexistence. Those profound events came at a moment in history when the human sciences had for some time been probing the calcified layers of cultural deposits that had built up concerning the nature of man. The social, behavioral and mental-health sciences had begun to hint that these simplified, visible surfaces, with their bland symmetry and synthetic construction, were false images of what man really was. We had already been shaken by these suggestions. The bold confrontation of Freud, for instance, had cut deep below the surface, even though we recoiled in disgust and indignation at what he claimed to have found. Then the flash at Hiroshima provided a light of such piercing intensity that the visual blinders of the make-believe civilization we had fashioned for ourselves were torn from our eyes; the light reflected deep within the inner layers of our being. The added visual assault of cordwood corpses, brilliantly engineered gas ovens, and the realistic efficiency of the organization for collection, reduction and reprocessing of individual human bodies overpowered our sensory apparatus. We experienced depths of horror and acknowledgement within ourselves that overflowed such terms as terror, agony, guilt and insight.

Now we are awakening to a new reality that comes from inside ourselves; a reality that accentuates the inadequacy of the external structures and standards we had built for ourselves. We are particularly scrutinizing the nuclear socializing structures, such as education, family, religion, social welfare and legal correction, that attempt to bind man and society into a single union. It is these structures that give man the picture of what he is supposed to be. They are the structures that induct man into cultural standards, shape him toward their ends, and regulate any departure from their norms. They are the forces that we can mobilize against any individual who overtly invalidates our picture of ourselves. They are the vehicles that attempt to ameliorate any dissonance between the self and the culture and move rapidly into action whenever we are threatened by the overtly expressed behaviors of others that may breach our disguise and reveal the resonating companion urges in ourselves.

We are asking ourselves about these interlocutor structures, which seem so out of contact with what man really is. They either shape or fail to reshape the monstrous forms that he can assume. We seem to have decided that if they are the cradle of the culture, they need repair. As repositories of lessons learned before our time, they have extracted the error and retained the distortions that led us down the path to Auschwitz and Hiroshima. Yet how can we determine the directions in which they should be renovated or renewed? They are the bearers of the history of our culture as well as the designers of our lives. Can we correct history? If we cannot correct history, where do we look for different models, different baselines?

The accumulation of our experiences over the recent generations, particularly as we have witnessed the crystallization of destruction in the form of our modern death machine, has opened us to another standard than that of the socializing structures and their cultural content. We are realizing that culture-producing structures and culture-indoctrinating machinery are artifacts of humanity and not humanity itself. We are beginning to suspect that we cannot look to them for the corrective, but must turn back and delve into humanity for an answer to their failure and to our own. The intensity of our recent shocking experiences is freeing us from these cultural artifacts and putting us in direct contact with the humanity in ourselves. Such profound personal experiences are validating the scientifically couched findings of the human sciences and assuring us that we may be on the right track in looking into ourselves for a way out. As a result, there is a subtle shift taking place in our base of reality testing. There is a tremulous movement from the criteria of environmental organizations and environmental things to psychological principles and content. We are witnessing a penetration of the psychological into the social organizations of the state. We are seeing man's inner content pouring outward and becoming a test of reality in his external environment. We are beginning to measure man's world by his psychological reality, rather than distort his psychology to conform to the tortured structures of his cultural reality.

After the debacle of Nazi Germany, we were brought face to face with the logical conclusion of and "final solution" to the equation of civilization that we had constructed. The equation contained the terms technological organization and displacement, and was balanced when it equaled programmed death. Within the context of the kind of objective reality we had created for ourselves, we now had the final solution to the unacceptables in our midst. Scapegoating, displacement, projection and denial were scientifically perfected, and could be carried to the point of physical destruction of sacrificial populations. It was now possible to be finally rid of all those parts of our humanity that we reject. We need not talk about "helping" the scapegoat; we need not even talk about "curing" him. We could now effectively and finally eliminate him. It was a logical and clean solution, the Nazi-programmed solution. With it, all men could be blended into a nondivergent community. Those who did not blend would simply be eliminated. The ones called mentally ill, called crippled and criminal, even the ones called non-Aryan. It was a logical and technical culmination of the directions the world had been taking. It was a rational solution. The final solution.

The first crude instrument of a final solution was Germany's politically engineered power complex, which devoted and deployed all the forces of the collective toward this final end. Here engineered death was dependent on the vissicitudes of a political apparatus. At Hiroshima, however, a greatly simplified and more perfect instrument was demonstrated. Engineered death was now made possible through a technological and precise tool that did not depend upon the exigencies of human organization. There was no world jubilation over this ultimate model of the displacement solution. Instead we were overcome with horror at our own creation. Through this creation, psychological death wishes could be instantly translated into physical fulfillment. Psychosocial scapegoating now had a physical correlate, and there was no guaranteed buffer of safety between the two. We could no longer practice fantasied destruction without risking the hardening of fantasy into technical reality. Hate now bore the real seeds of death. The psychological and the physical were now completely interchangeable.

Out of this condition has emerged an even more profound probability, a probability that makes hate almost untenable: strong death wishes against other groups will lead to our own death. The sequence of events triggered by destructive intent toward others can boomerang and end in our destruction. In destroying "them" we may literally destroy ourselves. The physical instrument for carrying out the mission of psychological hate is, for the present, out of control and can bring about our own death along with those we hate. Thus we face a condition of existence that is new and different from that which we knew prior to our psychological revelations and our operational perfection of human-initiated mass death. Former modes of collective and personal existence no longer seem tenable. We must therefore try to construct new bases for human tolerance and new modes of coexistence. Old choices have been closed to us.

The three converging streams — the blinding clarity of our insight that cut through our previous fantasies of ourselves, the transmutability of hate and rejection into destructive instruments, and the probings of the human sciences — have thrust the psychological base of society into the foreground of human life. Consequently, in developed countries it is the psychological foundations rather than the economic foundations that are now determining the course of social existence.

The Rise of Mental Health

With the end of World War II and the development of nuclear explosives, an epoch had ended. The ecology that existed was no longer the simple one of man's biological relations to his world. Now his psychological states had assumed an importance and urgency not heretofore accorded them. Psychological penetration into the physical world had occurred to the point where recognition and place in the order of things had to be made for it. Psychological events now had an immediacy and impact that could compete with physical events for the attention and resources of the community. This development led to the rise of a mental-health cult. The social, personal and cultural upheaval was being interpreted as a mere departure from normal, a deviation from some presumed state of health. Viewing it in this light, many interpreted it as an unfortunate derangement that could be healed and corrected, thus returning the world to a mythical state of normality. All had been reduced to a model of physical disease. The profound insights we had gained and the attendant personnel and social dislocations were distorted to fit this model. The problem was approached as though it represented an epidemic to be understood and corrected. We spoke of prevention and treatment as though a disease entity existed, a disease that could be inoculated against and subjected to the medical laboratory, the chemical agents and the hospital regime. We talked and acted as though we could transform the world into one big mental hospital, as though the ruptures of men's psychological characteristics through the constraining structures of his collective framework could be repaired with a little surgery and a little therapy. We acted as though our internal nature was sick, and we were in the process of returning it to a former state of health.

A Wider Perspective

It was not long, however, before the stirring and awakening began to express itself in so many facets and through so many growing tributaries that it soon overflowed the single new channel of mental health. Even though mental health, in its astounding growth and rallying focus, had burst forth in a brief decade as a fully developed social institution, the vast outpouring of human forces and human urgencies had soon swept it up along with the older socializing and humanizing agencies. It was obvious that the flood was greater than mental health and encompassed a horde of uprisings, human protests and revisions that could not be contained within that single concept. The confrontation with racial domination of the cultural system developed to maintain this domination, the confrontation between generation and the passionate protest of youth against the decisions and apparatus of the older controlling generation, the discovery of the poor and the convulsive efforts to change history by eliminating this cultural reality, the radical reversals in religious policy and religious dogma all spread far beyond this simple conception.

As a consequence an historical storm seems to be sweeping our lives. The world is wracked with violent heavings. In the midst of this turbulence it appears to be shifting its axis toward the human self and the full psychological reality of the self. In the shift it is almost as though humanity is trembling between the poles of renaissance and annihilation. We seem to be experiencing the intolerable agony of suspense between these two awesome possibilities. The storm has broken through the bounds of all existing crystallized conceptions of human existence. Exploding behavioral knowledge and technology are converging with imploding revelations of the inner nature of the human condition. These forces have exposed and erupted hidden secrets into our external environment, into the very cultural contexts we have created for collective living. Our daily lives and the cultural pathways open to them are being shaken and changed. Such culture-binding contexts as religion, law, family, education and social welfare are being profoundly affected and influenced by them. The relationship of group to group and person to person is being revised.

The basic socializing functions that our major institutions have served are being reexamined and the forms that these functions have taken are undergoing critical renovation. The social-welfare system, the legal-correctional system, the eduational system, the religious system, the family system are all in the midst of accelerated and provoked change. The social codes and cultural legends that they served are being challenged and criticized. In a sense, the culture itself is under seige. The established order, in all its forms, is being assaulted from divergent and frequently conflicting positions. Schools and the ideology of education, welfare programs and the ideology of social service, the correctional system and the legal ideology, churches and their ideologies are all receiving accusations and pressures for reform. This new wave washing over the lives of men seems to be uncontrolled or perhaps uncontrollable, except by some internal rhythm of historical movements, which, once set into motion, sweeps through every facet and territory of human existence. The dreamer, the man of action and the great mass of people to whom it is happening are all being swept along in its force. The very nature and condition of human existence is being changed in such a revolution.

An Interpretation

This upheaval in human affairs has been interpreted by one group of classicists as a situation of crisis. They see man as poised on the brink of a personal-social confrontation. They accept Freud's conception of the self as being discontinuous with the culture, not wholly created by the culture, and they see the standing quarrel and natural cleavage between self and culture as having reached a dangerous apex. Many years ago Freud summarized the nature of the critical situation as follows:

> The fateful question of the human species seems to me to be whether and to what extent the cultural processes developed in it will succeed in mastering the derangements of communal life caused by the human instinct of aggression and self destruction. In this connection, perhaps the phase through which we are at this moment passing deserves special interest. Men have brought forces of nature to such a pitch that by using them they could now very easily exterminate one another to the last man. They know this – hence arises a great part of their current unrest, their dejections, their mood of apprehension. And now it may be expected that the other of these two 'heavenly forces,' eternal Eros, will put forth his strength so as to maintain himself alongside his equally immortal adversary.[3]

[3] Freud, S. *Civilization and its discontents*. Translated by Joan Riviere. London: Hogarth Press, 1930, p. 143-144.

The state of affairs described by Freud in the late 1920s is perceived as prophetic by the modern classicists who have carried these themes further. Lionel Trilling stated what he considers to be the essence of our condition. He believes that we have reached a crisis in which the standing quarrel between self and culture demands urgent solution. In pointing up the crisis, he says:

> But it can sometimes happen that a culture intent upon giving the very highest value and honor to the selves that comprise it can proceed on its generous enterprise without an accurate awareness of what the self is, or what it may be. Such loss of accurate knowledge about the self it is possible to observe in our own culture at this time. It is, I believe, a very generous culture, and in its conscious thought it sets great store by the conditions of life which are manifestly appropriate to the self, and of the right relation of the self to the culture. This progressive deterioration of accurate knowledge of the self, and the right relation between the self and the culture constitutes what I am calling the crisis in our culture.[4]

This sense of crisis, of a time and circumstance that threaten to engulf and destroy man is echoed by Marcuse (1962) and Brown (1959).

Marcuse's theme is the high correlation between progress and unfreedom of the individual. He sees the domination of man by man as growing in scope and intensity throughout the world of industrial civilization:

> Nor does this trend appear as an incidental, transitory regression on the road to progress. Concentration camps, mass extermination, world wars, and atom bombs are no 'relapse into barbarism' but the unrepressed implementation of the achievement of modern science, technology, and domination. And the most effective subjugation and destruction of man by man takes place at the height of civilization, when the material and intellectual attainments of mankind seem to allow the creation of a truly free world.[5]

[4]Trilling, Lionel. *Freud and the crisis of our culture.* Boston: The Beacon Press, 1955, p. 33.

[5]*Ibid.*, p. 4.

Norman Brown addresses himself to the same profound ideas that concerned Trilling and Marcuse. In the introduction to his book *Life Against Death,* he claims that when our eyes are open, we experience our present situation in its full concrete actuality as a tragic crisis. It is apparent, he says, that with all man's restless striving and voicing of progress, he does not know what he really wants. Freud was right. Our real desires are unconscious, and because they are unconscious, we are unable to obtain satisfaction. As a consequence, we are hostile to life and ready to destroy ourselves. Freud was also right in positing a death instinct. Our current success in developing such efficient weapons of destruction make our dilemma quite clear: "We either come to terms with our unconscious instincts and drives — with life and with death — or else we surely die."[6]

Each of these authors sees man as bound and unfree. Their composite analysis suggests that man has created cultural structures to reinforce his bonds. He has tried not to acknowledge all that he is. He denies much of his being, and has set up cultural barriers to the expression of parts of this being. Culturally, he has relegated large territories within himself to nonexistence, to secret existence or to extrasocial existence. The result of centuries of attempted nonbeing has been the cumulative reinforcement of cultural channels and crystallized social structures that are frequently retaliatory, hostile and destructive. The culture is often hostile to the self. Out of this fact, out of cultural indoctrination, massive cultural warnings and fear of social retaliation, the individual is hostile to his selfhood.

A Particular Focus

The thesis presented in this book accepts much of this crisis interpretation. The book concerns itself, however,

[6]Brown, Norman O. *Life against death.* New York: Vintage Books, 1959, p. xiii.

with the ways that society has devised to try to bring order into the derangements of personal and social processes. It focuses particularly to the interlocutor processes and apparatuses of the community that have evolved to reconcile the claims of individual with the claims of society. These are the formal civilizing and acculturating instrumentalities of the modern community, which support and supplement the family processes of socialization.

This book looks at the self-denying and self-rejecting elements of socialization and the residual failures of these efforts. It investigates the way in which the interlocutor instrumentalities are drawn into this realm of human functioning. The argument is made that in spite of denial, rejection and cultural surveillance through the interlocutor mechanisms of behavior management, there are in each of us vast areas of the unacknowledged self, which has continued its socially alien, subterranean existence through the centuries. Our favored method of relief has been to acknowledge its existence in others who have been less sufficiently socialized. We obtain vicarious release by observing its manifestations in their behavior and then marshaling the interlocutor forces of the community to come to bear on these behaviors. It is proposed that this procedure falls hardest on the most vulnerable populations in society, but that we have come to a point in history where such displacement solutions are under reexamination as a consequence of recent historical events. The displacement-solution model was carried to the final, logical expression of its psychological intent in the socially engineered programs of Hitlerian Germany. The incisive conclusion followed shortly thereafter when the destructive apparatus achieved technological perfection in the atom bomb.

Now, in the time of confrontation and revision, it is necessary to look deeper into the collective psychology of behavioral threat and community response. We must pay particular attention to the institutionalized transactions associated with these collective expressions. The need to bring order into the derangements of personal and social processes is extremely urgent. A more logical and orderly means of behavior management must be devised as quickly as possible, and our present interlocutor tools must be radically modified in order to bring about a more equitable and satisfactory relationship between self and society before we destroy ourselves.

The present practices and institutions of behavior management are under a great strain as we go through this profound period of transition and change. Whether or not they are equal to the challenge of these times remains to be seen. We must begin to recognize, however, that these practices and institutions are integral to our survival and growth as human societies. We must begin to look at the pattern of diverse strategies and agencies for human regulation as instrumental means for the management of the man-made ecology of modern communities. If we manage the ecological conditions well, then both the individual and the community should flourish. If we manage them poorly, then we could be devastated by the processes at work within ourselves and our society.

Index

145